A CHORUS LINE
THE BOOK OF THE MUSICAL

A CHORUS LINE

Conceived, Choreographed and Directed by
Michael Bennett

Book by
James Kirkwood
Nicholas Dante

Music by
Marvin Hamlisch

Lyrics by
Edward Kleban

APPLAUSE
NEW YORK • LONDON

An Applause Original

A CHORUS LINE
Book Copyright © 1975, 1985, 1995
by James Kirkwood Trust, Michael Bennett, and Nicholas Dante
Music by Marvin Hamlish, Lyrics by Edward Kleban
Copyright © 1975, 1977, 1985, 1995 by Wren Music Company and American Compass Music Corp.
Preface Copyright © 1995 by Samuel G. Freedman
Introduction Copyright © 1995 by Frank Rich
Photographs Copyright © 1992 by Martha Swope
International Copyright secured.
All rights reserved.

Library of Congress Cataloging-in-Publication Data
Hamlisch, Marvin.
[Chorus line. Libretto]
A chorus line / conceived, choreographed and directed by Michael Bennett : book by James Kirkwood & Nicolas Dante:
music by Marvin Hamlisch: lyrics by Edward Kleban.
p. cm.
"An Applause original" T.p. verso.
ISBN 1-55783-131-9 :
1. Musicals–Librettos. I. Bennett, Michael, 1943 Apr. 8- II. Kirkwood, James, 1930-   III. Dante, Nicholas.
IV. Kleban, Edward. V. Title.
ML50.H2397C5   1995   <Case>
782.1'4'-0268–dc20

95-21617
CIP

Applause Theatre & Cinema Books
19 West 21st Street, Suite 201
New York, NY 10010
Phone: (212) 575-9265
Fax: (212) 575-9270
Email: info@applausepub.com
Internet: www.applausepub.com

Applause books are available through your local bookstore, or you may order at
www.applausepub.com or call Music Dispatch at 800-637-2852

Sales & Distribution
North America:
Hal Leonard Corp.
7777 West Bluemound Road
P. O. Box 13819
Milwaukee, WI 53213
Phone: (414) 774-3630
Fax: (414) 774-3259
Internet: www.halleonard.com
Email: halinfo@halleonard.com

PREFACE

Samuel G. Freedman

To understand the phenomenon of *A Chorus Line,* to appreciate the emotional appeal that made it the longest-running show in Broadway history, requires a kind of willful amnesia. One must strip away everything that has accreted around this musical—the nine Tony Awards, the Pulitzer Prize, the national and international tours, the record-breaking 3,389th performance, celebrated in Shubert Alley with 30 pounds of caviar and 35 cases of champagne. Even the unanimous raves that greeted *A Chorus Line* cannot explain its staying power, for in Manhattan, vogue has a half-life measured in months.

A Chorus Line earned its extravagant rewards, but from its first preview on April 16, 1975, to its final and 6,137th performance on April 28, 1990, it was never about stardom. Stardom excludes; stardom is a club of one. *A Chorus Line* did honor to struggle, struggle and possibility, two inclusive concepts. It is worth remembering that at the outset, long before it became the surest, safest brand name, *A Chorus Line* represented what one critic called "musical-verité," created by necessity outside Broadway and the commercial theater's conventions.

There is a particular value, too, to reminding ourselves of New York and its travails of a generation ago. That history provides more than newsreel backdrop; it provides context and clues.

During the late spring of 1975, New York City seemed to be dying a ghastly and self-inflicted death. The South Bronx, once a neighborhood that nurtured immigrant dreams, was burning with thirty fires a week. The public housing projects that had typified liberalism's social contract now bred the crime and despair of a burgeoning "underclass." With Albany and Washington refusing it emergency aid, with Wall Street loath to buy its bonds, New York teetered on the edge of bankruptcy. And to a large segment of America, there would be nothing less than divine justice in such a collapse, for this city, to quote just two detractors, suffered from "an overtone of sinfulness," "a terrific moral laxity."

In those horrible weeks, as broadcasts and newspapers carried each new calamity like a wartime bulletin, a different sort of buzz was coursing through the theater community. After sixteen months of obscure gestation, the new musical directed by Michael Bennett for Joseph Papp's New York Shakespeare Festival, the one called *A Chorus Line*, was playing previews. And, suddenly, the word was that it was something extraordinary. Night after night, the 299-seat house sold out, on one occasion leaving Liza Minelli to watch from an aisle step. Two producers offered $150,000 for the film rights, and were refused.

All that cachet, though, served to conceal the grittiness so central to the creation and enduring attraction of *A Chorus Line*. At the most basic level, the show's evolution through a series of low-paying workshops occurred only because Broadway was sharing the city's economic malaise. "In 1974, there wasn't other work," Bennett said bluntly of his original cast. "If there'd been work, they wouldn't have been at the Shakespeare Festival for $100 a week. No one's that noble."

More importantly, *A Chorus Line* conveyed the allure that New York, even in its most troubled and maligned moments, holds for creative and performing artists, and for those who revel in their accomplishments. If anything, the very traits of political liberalism and social tolerance that earn New York such scorn west of the Hudson have always drawn the most gifted and quirky and diverse refugees from the provinces. Like the Greek dramas that underlie all Western theater, *A Chorus Line* enacts a communal myth, the myth of finding acceptance and identity in an alien place that feels ineffably like home.

What is the term, after all, that Broadway show dancers have bestowed upon themselves? They are "gypsies," with all the itinerant and unsavory qualities the word suggests. In *A Chorus Line,* an audience meets them first as numbers, then as "boys" and "girls" in a director's condescending words, then as the eight-by-ten glossies they hold over their faces, and only lastly as individuals with names and stories. Of the 24 aspirants who audition for the unnamed musical-within-the-musical, only eight will be chosen, an attrition unthinkable in most Broadway confections. As Walter Kerr wrote shortly after the opening, *A Chorus*

Line "wants us to feel the happiness that overtakes these nonentities so long as toes slap the ground and fly into the air—at the same time we recognize the essential hopelessness of their lots."

The two dancers we come to know best and embrace most leave the stage, respectively, in tragedy and compromise. Paul, whose monologue about dancing in a drag show is the text's climax, crumples to the floor with a knee injury. Cassie wins a spot in the chorus, but with the audience knowing that she has returned in failure from California and the movies. "It would be nice to be a star," she says of her downward mobility. "But I'm not. I'm a dancer." Even the final sequence of "One," all sequins and top hats and tails, a scene that appears to clutch the kitsch the rest of the show abhors, struck Bennett more darkly. "That finale is so sad," he told the author Ken Mandelbaum. "The craft is wonderful, but you ask, did they go through all that just to be anonymous?"

Anonymity, though, is not the least of *A Chorus Line*'s attributes. Even the most ardent theatregoer would be pressed now, 21 years after the show debuted, to name its entire creative team—Bennett, authors Nicholas Dante and James Kirkwood, lyricist Ed Kleban, composer Marvin Hamlisch, and choreographer Bob Avian. Only one song from the score, the torchy "What I Did For Love," entered the pop repertory. None of the original cast's performers gained the stardom their Tony Awards seemed to prophecy. By the mid-1980s, Sammy Williams, the original Paul, found himself working in a flower shop. Donna McKechnie, very much like the Cassie she portrayed, went to Hollywood only to wind up directing pro football cheerleaders. Both ultimately returned to their roles in *A Chorus Line.* And the inability of these talented individuals to surpass their collective achievement attests not only to the chemistry of *A Chorus Line* on stage but to its very origins.

As recounted in Mandelbaum's authoritative book, *A Chorus Line and the Musicals of Michael Bennett,* the project began with an offer by two disgruntled Broadway gypsies, Tony Stevens and Michon Peacock, to gather a group of dancers for a rap session with Bennett. Once a chorus boy himself, but by early 1974 a major choreographer and director with such credits as *Company* and *Follies,* Bennett already had the inchoate idea of developing a theater piece about show dancers. He would later attribute *A Chorus Line* to his revulsion at the Watergate scandal, but Donna McKechnie may have struck closer to the essence when she suggested that Bennett, in creating the musical, was "longing for the innocence, the pure expression of just going in there and working, backing up the star, dishing with the guys, having flirtations, standing in the back and saying, 'God, I'm better than that director.'"

So, at midnight on January 18, 1974, some 24 dancers met with Bennett in a rehearsal studio on East 23rd Street. For the next twelve hours, and again a few weeks later, they danced and talked and ate and talked and drank and talked, with a tape recorder capturing every revelation. The group included eight members of the original cast, among them McKechnie and Williams, as well as the show's initial author, Nicholas Dante, whose account of his time in the Jewel Box Revue became Paul's soliloquy in the finished show.

Still, it diminishes the achievement of *A Chorus Line* to imply, as theater legend often has, that creating the show simply involved editing a few transcripts and setting them to song. More than specific anecdotes, the gypsies supplied verisimilitude. These young men and women had grown up in backwaters like Byhalia, Mississippi, and Royal Oak, Michigan, and Arlington, Vermont, dreaming of dance and Manhattan. What they found there was not spotlight stardom but faceless gigs in Radio City and on "Hullabaloo" and the endless anxiety of auditions for work on a dwindling Broadway. They spoke of torn cartilage and cosmetic surgery and unemployment lines, the realities of their lives. And by remaining faithful to the peculiarities of that narrow world, Bennett and his collaborators let true universality emerge. "There is *truth* on that stage," he later would say. "Nothing monumental or astounding, but truth nonetheless."

But that gets ahead of the story. After Stevens and Peacock failed to develop a project from the tapes, Bennett bought the rights from the participating dancers. (He gave all of them and other members of the original cast a share in any subsidiary income that he might derive from

A Chorus Line, which a few sought to increase once the show became a hit.) Through the summer of 1974, Bennett and Dante started to shape the material, with composer Marvin Hamlisch and lyricist Ed Kleban joining the enterprise. That August, Papp agreed to pay for a workshop of the nascent show, despite the fact his theater was $1.5 million in debt. The first workshop gave way to a second, with the playwright James Kirkwood now coming aboard as Dante's co-author. Even during the famously successful previews, Bennett continued to tinker, drawing on uncredited script doctors and worrying his cast into accepting extra rehearsals. By the time the process ended, Papp had spent $500,000 and he and Bennett had changed the entire way of making musical theater.

The center of gravity for new dramatic writing had already begun shifting from Broadway to an array of nonprofit theaters by the mid-1970s. But the musical, the big, hit musical, was still considered the commercial theater's bailiwick. So much of those musicals' lore, in fact, arose from the pressured process of reaching Broadway—the backers' audition with Jerry Bock and Sheldon Harnick accompanying themselves on the score to *The Old Country,* later renamed *Fiddler on the Roof;* the out-of-town try-out with Stephen Sondheim writing "Comedy Tonight" while *A Funny Thing Happened on the Way to the Forum* was in Washington. *A Chorus Line* demonstrated that a musical, especially a daring one, could grow better within the twin shelters of the workshop arrangement and the institutional theater. The old wisdom shifted, especially as the cost of mounting a new musical rose toward the current benchmark of nearly $15 million. The commercial musical has hardly gone extinct, of course, and the nonprofit method has rarely worked as well or as purely as it did for Bennett and Papp. Yet it is impossible to imagine how *Sunday in the Park with George* or *Falsettos* or *Big River* could have played on Broadway without having followed the route *A Chorus Line* pioneered.

And as a prolifically bountiful cash cow, *A Chorus Line* largely supported the Shakespeare Festival for years, yielding $37.8 million in profits as of February 1990, the most recent accounting. In a financial syllogism, those monies helped pay for the artistically rewarding and fiscally dubious ventures to follow—dramas by Vaclav Havel and David Hare, summer after summer of Shakespeare in Central Park, musicals from Galt MacDermot and Elizabeth Swados. Those shows represent a more lasting, more enriching, more significant ripple effect from *A Chorus Line* than the companies that trekked to Singapore and Norway and Argentina.

It is both ironic and appropriate that *A Chorus Line* lived most of its life on Broadway, the same Broadway the show celebrated and rebelled against. Bennett, Kirkwood, Dante, Kleban, Hamlisch, and Avian all were children of the commercial theater. Part downtown iconoclast, Papp equally embodied the classic impresario. He showed nothing but old-style Broadway moxie by announcing *A Chorus Line*'s final performance for March 31, 1990, thus stirring up enough business to squeeze out 33 more.

And in each of those final audiences, one can be sure, sat some teenager from a small town or a boring suburb or a dangerous slum, some teenager dreaming of escape and expression and that stage, that stage. For true believers, from Moss Hart to Madonna, no amount of trash or strife or crime can sully the promise of New York, the promise that *A Chorus Line* will always evoke. As the gypsy named Bebe puts it, "I don't wanna hear about how Broadway's dying. 'Cause I just got here."

Samuel G. Freedman covered theater for *The New York Times* from 1983 through 1986, reporting on the record-breaking, 3,389th performance of *A Chorus Line* and writing often about Michael Bennett and Joseph Papp. He is the author of *Small Victories: The Real World of a Teacher, Her Students & Their High School,* which was a finalist for the 1990 National Book Award, *Upon This Rock: The Miracles of a Black Church,* and the forthcoming *The Inheritance: How Three Families and America Moved from Roosevelt to Reagan and Beyond.*

INTRODUCTION
Frank Rich

It is hard to believe that almost twenty years have passed since *A Chorus Line* first electrified a New York audience. The memories of the show's birth in 1975, not to mention those of its 15-year life and poignant death, remain incandescent—and not just because nothing so exciting has happened to the American musical since. For a generation of theater people and theatergoers, *A Chorus Line* was and is the touchstone that defines the glittering promise, more often realized in legend than in reality, of the Broadway theater.

The show's birth, so widely documented that it has long since taken on the dimensions of a fable, came after a celebrated gestation conducted by the director-choreographer Michael Bennett in workshops at Joseph Papp's Public Theater Off Broadway. The first performances of *A Chorus Line*, unheralded and virtually unadvertised, created such a spontaneous forest fire of word-of-mouth that the show became a hit instantaneously, well before the critics' raves or the avalanche of accompanying publicity turned a local phenomenon into a national one.

But *A Chorus Line* was not just a hit in the old Broadway sense, and it departed in distinct ways from *My Fair Lady* and *Hello, Dolly!* and *Fiddler on the Roof*, the classics whose records it would eventually smash. *A Chorus Line* was not developed in a pre-Broadway tryout in New Haven or Philadelphia or Washington but in a 299-seat non-profit theater in the East Village. And though *A Chorus Line*'s subject was Broadway, it did not trade in the nostalgic glamour of Broadway so familiar from old-time backstage musicals and movies. *A Chorus Line* found its life in the workaday routine of the theatre. Its drama originated in the tough, ordinary lives of unsung chorus people auditioning and even begging for jobs (sometimes with dignity, sometimes not) that offered no hope of stardom or even financial security.

This was hardly the typical stuff—and setting—of a hit Broadway musical. *A Chorus Line* had no marching bands with 76 trombones, no Dolly Levi descending a glittering red staircase, no Cecil

Beaton tableaus of elegant Edwardian society, no galvanic gang wars between the Jets and Sharks. In fact, *A Chorus Line* took place in a plain black box, an empty stage, with its most conspicuous "scenery" being a white line painted across the downstage floor and a row of mirrors that would occasionally twirl into view against the rear wall. And at its center there was no Channing or Merman or Martin or Preston but quite the contrary: performers whose only professional mission was to dance anonymously in the shadows behind such a star in the unnamed musical for which they were auditioning.

What made this work so fascinating to its audiences will be in part apparent from the pages that follow. Inspired by tapes of informal sessions in which a group of long-time Broadway dancers recounted their battle scars, frustrations, heartbreaks, fears and small triumphs, the authors James Kirkwood and Nicholas Dante take the audience on a documentary survey of a Broadway chorus performer's existence. As the characters of *A Chorus Line* deliver autobiographical monologues to the director, Zach, the audience learns of the unhappy childhoods that often drove them to dream of escaping into the theater, of the pleasures and humiliations that greeted them once they realized their dreams, and of the physical and psychological wear-and-tear that inevitably end dancers' careers at a relatively young age. The faceless and forgotten veterans of the hard-scrabble showbiz life become vividly human in *A Chorus Line*. Along the way, one also picks up a certain amount of inside information about how the backstage business of Broadway actually works, and of how Broadway musicals are assembled at the grunt level. *A Chorus Line* was also the first Broadway musical to deal matter-of-factly with homosexuality, and from an inside point-of-view that makes its gay men, the tortured Paul aside, seem far more accessible than the martyrs and oddballs that typified stage homosexuals in mainstream American drama of the post-*Boys In the Band*, pre-AIDS era.

But *A Chorus Line* is not journalism, not an oral history, not a documentary. Though the Kirkwood-Dante book for the show is based loosely on true life stories, the characters are often composites, their words often fictionalized and reinvented as stage dialogue. The same is also the case, obviously, with Edward Kleban's lyrics, which ingeniously weave several dancers' stories together in a poetically heightened song like "At the Ballet" or which mock Broadway clichés in the big number the dancers must learn as part of their audition, "One." If the script of *A Chorus Line* were merely a Studs Terkel-esque assemblage of eyewitness testimony, there is no way the show could have caused the excitement that it did, or that it could have earned the international longevity it enjoyed. Backstage tales, however frank, lose their novelty soon enough, and are hardly the basis for a musical so wide in appeal that it became the longest running production in Broadway history once it moved from the Public to the Shubert Theater in the summer of '75.

Though the broad popularity of *A Chorus Line* has often been attributed to its we-are-all-in-a-chorus-line universality, I would argue that it is the originality of its style, not the low common denominator of its theme, that really made it ignite. As befits a show set in the theater, it is the theatricality of *A Chorus Line* that counts most. Unlike any hit Broadway musical before it, *A Chorus Line* was celebrated as much for its presentation of its content as for the content itself. With all due respect to Marvin Hamlisch's inventive score, few would mention it in the same breath as the classic scores that figured in the comparable hit Broadway musicals of Rodgers and Hammerstein, Lerner and Loewe, or Frank Loesser. Nor would anyone liken the book of *A Chorus Line*, either in its dramatic construction or pathos or wit, to those of, say, *My Fair Lady* or *Guys and Dolls* or *Gypsy*. Nor can the success of *A Chorus Line* be attributed to its original cast (which was superb, but not indelible or, as it turned out, irreplaceable), its production design or even a show-stopping dance number.

Rather, it was the stitching together of all its elements in that purest of theatrical arenas, a deep and empty stage, by its director-choreographer that made *A Chorus Line* so thrilling to its audience. Michael Bennett did not take a more-or-less finished script and then merely edit and direct it—the role played by directors in most other classic American musicals—but reversed the process. He began with an idea (inspired by those famous tapes) and then had the show written over the course of its lengthy workshop development period to correspond to his own vision of what it should be. That vision was based not only on the conviction that chorus performers' stories demanded to be heard but also on the notion that a story could be told on stage through continuous movement inseparable from dialogue and songs. While *A Chorus Line* had remarkably little dancing, especially for a show about dancers, it could be said that the entire show was danced: its performers kept moving back and forth in different patterns through the depth of the stage, forever splintering and then reconstituting their chorus line. It was as if the company were one giant, undulating organism forever torn between the shadows of the wings and the footlights down front. The dancers' bodies and Tharon Musser's elaborate lighting plot became, in essence, the musical's scenery, replacing the turntables of illustrative scenery that had been *de rigeur* in Broadway's past classical musicals.

Bennett did not invent this brand of musical-theater storytelling. *A Chorus Line* built on the innovations of Agnes de Mille, who first used dancers to act out characters' hidden emotions in the Rodgers-and-Hammerstein *Oklahoma!* (1943), and those of Jerome Robbins, whose staging of the musicals *West Side Story* (1957) and *Fiddler on the Roof* (1964) contained long sequences in which the fluidity of movement, song, and drama was unbroken. Bennett had refined these techniques in his most important pre-*Chorus Line* projects, *Company* (1970) and *Follies* (1971), both of them collaborations with the director Harold Prince, whose own innovative approach to musical theater reflected his association with Robbins as the producer of both *West Side Story* and *Fiddler*.

Even so, in *A Chorus Line*, Bennett took this method of musical-theater storytelling further than anyone had before. Though Robbins had played a strong part in shaping the materials of his musicals to his own theatrical ideas, it would still be impossible to imagine *West Side Story* without the Leonard Bernstein-Stephen Sondheim songs or *Fiddler* without the central image of Tevye (whether Sholom Aleichem's or Zero Mostel's). In *A Chorus Line*, the show as an entity was a star. Never had a director-choreographer played such a dominant role in the creation of a musical as Bennett did with *A Chorus Line*. (Indeed, Bennett's painstaking, organic creation of the show at the Public over months of trial-and-error could not have been done within the budget and time limitations of the Broadway system.) Never had the usual accouterments of the Broadway musical, starting with the star system and an elaborate physical production, been thrown out to pursue this goal of theatrical seamlessness. And never had a Broadway musical achieved such a continuous stream of movement on all theatrical fronts in its finished version. Though *A Chorus Line* occasionally stands still—as in "What I did for Love," its big ballad and most conventional fixture—it is usually typified by the multi-track rush of activity (song, dialogue, dance, lighting, underscoring) in numbers like "I Hope I Get It" and the 15-minute-long "Hello Twelve, Hello Thirteen, Hello Love." As both written and staged, these numbers tell the stories of nearly two-dozen characters simultaneously and in a manner far psychologically richer and more dramatic than the lyrics, or the original-cast album, can suggest in isolation. Stage devices resembling such cinematic devices as the dissolve, the wipe, the close-up, and the montage are all executed by means of lighting, choreography, and staging. And even the film parallels do not do complete justice to the magic Bennett achieved in the flesh. It is because the director's techniques made so much exhilarating use of stage space and abstract movement that their indigenously theatrical effect defied translation in the deadly Hollywood screen adaptation of *A Chorus Line*. They also defy replication in a script's stage directions.

Unsurprisingly, Bennett's instinctive genius for the theater never crossed over into another medium; while the success of *Chorus Line* brought him Hollywood contracts and projects, he never directed a movie. Before his death at age 44 in 1987, he had shown signs of stretching the esthetic achievement of *A Chorus Line* in new directions on the Broadway stage. *Dreamgirls*, his hit of 1981, was even more flamboyant in its manipulation of bodies, space, narrative, and nonrepresentational scenic elements. Using mobile towers of nearly Constructivist design, Mr. Bennett propelled his characters (a trio of Supreme-like pop singers) through decades of personal and cultural history and a myriad of interior and exterior locales without ever using a literal setting (or even much dialogue).

In September, 1983, Bennett scored another coup when he restaged *A Chorus Line* for a single night—the night of its record-breaking 3,389th Broadway performance—to accommodate the more than 300 cast alumni he wanted to include in the gala celebration. Rather than jazzing up the original staging of the show, he rethought, rechoreographed, and sometimes deconstructed the original scenes to leave an emotionally overwhelmed audience with the feeling that any future was possible in the daring theater of Michael Bennett.

At this writing, that future has not happened. It was in part another casualty of AIDS, which killed Bennett, whose memorial service would be conducted on the Shubert stage four years to the day after the gala for performance 3,389. Of the original *Chorus Line* creators, Kleban and Kirkwood also failed to outlive their own creation. Dante died a year after *A Chorus Line*'s 1990 closing. Papp, perhaps the only producer in the New York theater with the guts to subsidize extravagant experimentation by artists as ambitious as Bennett, died in 1991.

No successor to Bennett has yet emerged. Though some of the successful London musicals, from *Cats* to *Les Miserables*, draw on both the Bennett and Robbins innovations, none of them has added anything new to the mix. And though everyone in the theater concedes that lengthy workshops might be the best way to develop new musicals as original as *A Chorus Line*, no commercial producer or non-profit company has the combination of patience and cash needed to give artists the time and unequivocal support Papp gave Bennett.

Within two seasons after *A Chorus Line*'s departure from the Shubert in 1990, the Broadway musical showed signs of retreat from the kind of seamless musical that director-choreographers like Robbins and Bennett had envisioned. The big hits of the 1991-92 season—*Guys and Dolls, Crazy for You,* and *Jelly's Last Jam*—all divided the duties of director and choreographer into separate jobs and, with the occasional exception of *Jelly's* (whose designer was the Bennett collaborator Robin Wagner), they all revived the pre-Robbins Broadway musical of the '40s and '50s in which book scenes and musical numbers alternate instead of marching forward in a single concentrated rush.

A *Chorus Line* itself, of course, persists in countless stock, amateur, and touring productions. But none of these versions can reproduce the original staging verbatim. Bennett's talent, like so much of what happens in the theater, was evanescent. His direction of A *Chorus Line* is inevitably diluted by the memories of those who recreate it and one day will fade entirely.

Yet such was and is the impact of A *Chorus Line* on its audiences, and on the hundreds of young theater people who passed through its many companies, that it still may prove more than a singular sensation. In its text, A *Chorus Line* stands for the supremacy of the individual, for the right of even the lowliest member of an ensemble to have his own integrity and dreams. In the theater, as realized by its director, A *Chorus Line* stood for the unlimited possibilities inherent in the blank slate of an empty stage. One can only guess how many of its alumni and rapt fans have been drawn into entering the creative process, particularly that of the theater, by its alluring example. The next generation's A *Chorus Line*, whatever it may be, could well come along because someone touched by this liberating musical felt, as one of its characters sings, "I Can Do That." The challenge for the American theater is to find and recognize these young talents, and, as Joseph Papp did for Michael Bennett and company, to give them a home away from the regimented Broadway chorus line where their imaginations can run free.

—Frank Rich
  August, 1994

A CHORUS LINE

A Chorus Line was originally presented by the New York Shakespeare Festival (Joseph Papp, producer) at the Newman Theater, New York City, April 15, 1975–July 13, 1975, for 101 performances. The New York Shakespeare Festival production, Joseph Papp, producer in association with Plum Productions, transferred to the Sam S. Shubert Theater, New York City, July 27, 1975, where it played 6,137 performances, closing April 28, 1990.

Conceived, Choreographed and Directed by Michael Bennett

Co-choreographer, Bob Avian

Setting by Robin Wagner

Costumes by Theoni V. Aldredge

Lighting by Tharon Musser

Sound by Abe Jacob

Orchestrations by Bill Byers, Hershey Kay & Jonathan Tunick

Music Coordinator, Robert Thomas

Musical Direction and Vocal Arrangements by Don Pippin

Original Cast

ROY ....Scott Allen
KRISTINE ....Renee Baughman
SHEILA ....Carole Bishop
VAL...Pamela Blair
MIKE ....Wayne Cilento
BUTCH...Chuck Cissel
LARRY ....Clive Clerk
MAGGIE ....Kay Cole
RICHIE ....Ronald Dennis
TRICIA ....Donna Drake
TOM ....Brandt Edwards
JUDY ....Patricia Garland
LOIS ....Carolyn Kirsch
DON..Ron Kuhlman
BEBE ....Nancy Lane
CONNIE ....Baayork Lee
DIANA...Priscilla Lopez
ZACH ....Robert LuPone
MARK ....Cameron Mason
CASSIE ....Donna McKechnie
AL ....Don Percassi
FRANK...Michael Serrecchia
GREG ....Michel Stuart
BOBBY ....Thomas J. Walsh
PAUL..Sammy Williams
VICKI ....Crissy Wilzak

Musical Numbers

"I Hope I Get It" ....Company

"I Can Do That" ....Mike

"And . . ." ....Bobby, Richie, Val, Judy

"At the Ballet" ....Sheila, Bebe, Maggie

"Sing!" ....Kristine, Al

"Hello Twelve, Hello Thirteen, Hello Love" ....Company

"Nothing" ....Diana

"Dance: Ten; Looks: Three" ....Val

"The Music and the Mirror" ....Cassie

"One" ....Company

"The Tap Combination" ....Company

"What I Did for Love" ....Diana and Company

"One" (Reprise) ....Company

An Audition

The Time: 1975

The Place: A Broadway Theater

The stage is completely bare, surrounded in black. There is a white line paint-ed on the floor downstage parallel to the footlights. The house goes to "half"— then to black. A rehearsal piano is heard. As the stage lights come up, we see three lines of dancers in rehearsal clothes, facing dance mirrors upstage. (The upstage wall is made of three-sided revolving panels. One side black, one side mirror and one side the special ribbon deco design used in the finale only.) In front of the dancers ZACH *is teaching a dance routine. A final audition is in progress.* LARRY *is assisting* ZACH. *Music is continuous under as* ZACH *instructs the dancers.*

ZACH: Again,
    Step, kick, kick, leap, kick, touch . . . Again!
    Step, kick, kick, leap, kick, touch . . . Again!
    Step, kick, kick, leap, kick, touch . . . Again!
    Step, kick, kick, leap, kick, touch . . . Right!
    That connects with . . .
    Turn, turn, out, in, jump, step,
    Step, kick, kick, leap, kick, touch.
    Got it? . . . Going on. And . . .
    Turn, turn, touch, down, back, step,
        (Beat)
    Five, six, seven, eight!
    Turn, turn, touch, down, back, step,
        (Beat)
    Five, six, seven, eight!
    Turn, turn, touch, down, back, step,
    Pivot, step, walk, walk, walk.
    The last part is . . .
    Pivot, step, walk, walk, walk.
    Reviewing from the last turn
    Five, six, seven, eight!

Turn, turn, touch, down, back, step,
Pivot, step, walk, walk, walk.
Right! Let's do the whole combination, facing away from the mirror. From the top, A-five, six, seven, eight!

> (*The music builds into full orchestration as the dancers face downstage and do the jazz combination with* ZACH *in front. When the combination is over, he crosses downstage right, near his stool. He speaks . . .*)

Okay, let's do the ballet combination one more time. Boys and girls together. Don't kill yourselves. Mark. A-*one*, two, three, *four*, five, six!

> (LARRY *demonstrates the combination downstage center. They mark the combination in various degrees. At one point* SHEILA *stops dancing and crosses stage right, exchanging a look with* ZACH; *reaching her dance bag, she brushes her hair. The others finish the ballet combination stage right.* LARRY *crosses to stool and gets audition cards and hands them to* ZACH *four at a time during the following*)

Okay, I'm going to put you into your groups now. When I call out your number, I'll tell you where you're gonna be in the formation.

JUDY (*Stepping out of the group*): Oh, God, I don't remember my number.

ZACH: Right, when I find a number without a person, it's you.

> (JUDY *backs into group*)

Okay, girls first. Number Two, downstage. (*He indicates their spot as he calls each number*) Number Nine, upstage. Number Ten, downstage. And number Twenty-three, upstage. Twenty-three? Judy Turner.

JUDY: Twenty-three. (*She runs into place*)

ZACH: Stage left, girls. Second group. Number Thirty-seven, down-stage. Number Sixty, upstage . . .

> (*The lights change to "internal thought" lighting as* ZACH *goes into pantomime. He continues to form groups. The others sing, excepting* CASSIE, *who does not sing in the opening number*)

ALL:
> GOD, I HOPE I GET IT.
> I HOPE I GET IT.
> HOW MANY PEOPLE DOES HE NEED?

BOYS:
> HOW MANY PEOPLE DOES HE NEED?

GIRLS:
> GOD, I HOPE I GET IT.

ALL:
> I HOPE I GET IT.
> HOW MANY BOYS, HOW MANY GIRLS?

GIRLS:
> HOW MANY BOYS, HOW MANY . . . ?

ALL:
> LOOK AT ALL THE PEOPLE!
> AT ALL THE PEOPLE.
> HOW MANY PEOPLE DOES HE NEED?
> HOW MANY BOYS, HOW MANY GIRLS?
> HOW MANY PEOPLE DOES HE . . . ?

TRICIA (*Warming-up downstage left*):

Above, girls' ballet: MAGGIE (Kay Cole), DIANA (Priscilla Lopez), JUDY (Patricia Garland) and KRISTINE (Renee Baughman); *below*, boys' ballet: Mark (Cameron Mason), MIKE (Wayne Cilento), GREG (Michel Stuart) and BOBBY (Thomas J. Walsh)

I REALLY NEED THIS JOB.
PLEASE, GOD, I NEED THIS JOB.
I'VE GOT TO GET THIS JOB.

> (*The lights change back to reality.* ZACH *comes out of pantomime . . .*)

ZACH: Third group of boys. Number Sixty-three downstage. Number Sixty-seven, upstage. Number Eighty-one, downstage. And number Eighty-four, upstage. Okay, boys, stage left. Let's do the ballet combination. First group of girls, second group follows. *One,* two, three, *four,* five, six . . .

> (*He crosses down to the bottom of the aisle stage right with* LARRY. *The first group of girls begins the ballet combination*)

Diana, you're dancing with your tongue again.

DIANA: Sorry . . . (*She falls out of turn*) Shit.

> (*First group of girls finishes the combination*)

ZACH: Next group . . . and . . .

> (*Second group of girls begins the combination stage right. To* VICKI)

You! Any ballet?

VICKI: No.

ZACH: Don't dance . . . DON'T DANCE!

> (VICKI *falls out of group, crosses right. The other three finish the combination*)

Next group, and . . .

> (*The third group of girls does the ballet combination.* TRICIA *dances so big, she winds up in front of* SHEILA—SHEILA *doesn't like that*)

Boys! And . . . Up . . . up . . . up . . .

> (*First group of boys begins the combination.* ZACH *comes onto the stage*)

Hold it. Hold it. Stop! (*To* ROY) How many years ballet?

ROY: One.

ZACH: Any Broadway shows?

ROY (*Shakes his head*): No.

ZACH (*Demonstrates to* ROY): The arms *are* second, down, fourth. I wanna see it. Again. *One*, two, three, *four*, five, six . . .

> (*First group of boys completes the combination.* ROY *continues to make same mistakes.* ZACH *goes back down to aisle*)

Next group:
And . . .

> (*Second group of boys begins combination. To* FRANK)

Boy in the headband, keep your head up. Headband, head up!

> (FRANK *looks at* ZACH, *appears to acknowledge his instruction, but continues to look down. Second group finishes combination*)

And . . .

> (*Third group of boys begins combination*)

Up! Up! Up!

> (*Third group of boys finishes combination. The lights change;* ZACH *goes onto the stage and into pantomime. As the group sings,* MAGGIE *{in pantomime} asks* ZACH *to demonstrate a part of the jazz combination. The first group of girls takes position.* ZACH *demonstrates . . .*)

ALL:

> GOD, I REALLY BLEW IT!
> I REALLY BLEW IT!
> HOW COULD I DO A THING LIKE THAT?

BOYS:

> HOW COULD I DO A THING LIKE . . .

ALL:

> NOW I'LL NEVER MAKE IT!
> I'LL NEVER MAKE IT!
> HE DOESN'T LIKE THE WAY I LOOK.
> HE DOESN'T LIKE THE WAY I DANCE.
> HE DOESN'T LIKE THE WAY I . . .

> (*The lights return to reality.* ZACH *goes back down to aisle. First group of girls dances the jazz combination. When they are finished . . .*)

ZACH (*To* KRISTINE): Girl in brown, much better but still too much tension face, neck and shoulders. Relax.

> (*Second group of girls is in position*)

Five, six, seven, eight . . .

> (VICKI *waves frantically to* ZACH)

Hold it! Hold it!

VICKI: I think I know the steps but could you have someone do it in front, please?

ZACH: Larry . . .

> (LARRY *takes a position down right of the group*)

Five, six, seven, eight.

Photo by Martha Swope

Boys' jazz combination: TOM (Brandt Edwards), RICHIE (Ronald Dennis), FRANK (Michael Serrecchia) and PAUL (Sammy Williams)

(*They dance with* LARRY. *When finished,* LARRY *goes back to aisle*)

Next group. A-five, six, seven, eight . . . (*To* VAL, *who is dancing behind* SHEILA *and not in her spot*) Dance out . . . Dance out! (*He goes up on stage. To group.*) Hold it. Hold it. Stop! (*To* SHEILA) Sheila, do me a favor, you dance upstage. (*To* VAL) You downstage.

(SHEILA *condescendingly gives up the front spot to* VAL)

A-five, six, seven, eight!

(ZACH *goes back to aisle. They do the combination. At one point,* SHEILA *misses the turns and tries to get back into the combination. She gives up and walks off as the girls dance off*)

Sheila, do you know the combination?

SHEILA: I knew it when I was in the front.

ZACH: Okay, first group of boys. A-five, six, seven, eight!

(*They start the combination.* AL *and* BUTCH *both make different mistakes*)

Hold it, hold it, stop! (*He goes back up to stage, demonstrates. To* AL) The step is, down step, pivot step. Not pivot step, pivot step, right? You chewing gum? Get rid of it.

(AL *runs stage right and gives his gum to* KRISTINE, *then returns to his position in the group, while* ZACH *talks to* BUTCH)

It's step, step, up, cross, turn from there . . . Okay, got it? Again. Five, six, seven, eight!

(*They complete the combination.* AL *corrects his mistake . . .* BUTCH *does not.* ZACH *goes to stage left, watches*)

Next group. A-five, six, seven, eight!

(*Second group of boys begins the combination.* RICHIE *leaps out of the formation in front of* PAUL. ZACH, *who has started to cross back to aisle, catches him in midair. To* RICHIE)

Listen, that's really great, but stay in the formation and tone it down. Okay? Boy in the headband, keep your head up. A-five, six, seven, eight . . .

(ZACH *goes back to aisle. They complete the combination*)

Next group. A-five, six, seven, eight.

(*Third group of boys dances the combination perfectly—end of combination overlaps with the beginning of vocal—and goes stage right with others.* ZACH *and* LARRY *come up on stage during the following. The lights change*)

ALL:
I REALLY NEED THIS JOB.
PLEASE, GOD, I NEED THIS JOB.
I'VE GOT TO GET THIS JOB.

(*Lights change back to reality.* ZACH *is upstage center*)

ZACH (*To* VICKI): Any Broadway shows?

VICKI (*Stepping forward*): No.

ZACH (*To* TRICIA): Broadway shows?

TRICIA (*Stepping forward*): Touring company.

ZACH: Okay, I'm eliminating down. When I call out your number, please form a line. Girls first. Number Two—

(DIANA *steps forward.* LARRY *indicates where she should stand*)

Number Nine, number Ten, number Twenty-three, Judy Turner? Right. Number Thirty-seven, One-hundred forty-nine, One hundred fifty-two, One-hundred seventy-nine . . . Cassie.

Photo by Martha Swope

ZACH (Robert LuPone) and LARRY (Clive Clerk)

(CONNIE, KRISTINE, JUDY, BEBE, MAGGIE, SHEILA *step out and form a line with* DIANA. VAL *goes to* SHEILA *then decides to cross to end of line next to* DIANA. CASSIE *steps out and stands next to* SHEILA)

Other girls. Thank you very much for coming. I'm sorry.

(*The girls who were eliminated exit up right*)

Boys. Number Five.

(AL *steps out and starts a line behind the girls*)

Number Seventeen, number Forty-four, Forty-five, Sixty-three, Sixty-seven, Eighty-one and Eighty-four.

(DON, RICHIE, PAUL, MARK, MIKE, GREG *and* BOBBY *step out and form a line with* AL)

Other boys, thank you.

(*The other boys exit up right*)

Larry . . .

(LARRY *crosses to* ZACH *as the lights change and . . .*)

ALL (*Plus all offstage voices*):
GOD, I THINK I'VE GOT IT.
I THINK I'VE GOT IT.
I KNEW HE LIKED ME ALL THE TIME.

ZACH: I want your pictures and resumes, please.

(*He goes up aisle to his desk in the back of the theatre. The group breaks up and goes to their dance bags to get pictures as . . .*)

ALL:
STILL IT ISN'T OVER.

MAGGIE:

WHAT'S COMING NEXT?

ALL:

IT ISN'T OVER.

MIKE:

WHAT HAPPENS NOW?

ALL:

I CAN'T IMAGINE WHAT HE WANTS.

GIRLS:

I CAN'T IMAGINE WHAT HE . . .

ALL:

GOD, I HOPE I GET IT!

I HOPE I GET IT.

>*(The group gathers center stage around* LARRY *who indicates that they should form a single line upstage)*

I'VE COME THIS FAR, BUT EVEN SO

IT COULD BE YES, IT COULD BE NO,

HOW MANY PEOPLE DOES HE . . . ?

I REALLY NEED THIS JOB.

A FEW VOICES:

MY UNEMPLOYMENT IS GONE.

ALL:

PLEASE, GOD, I NEED THIS JOB.

A FEW VOICES:

I KNEW I HAD IT FROM THE START.

CONNIE (Baayork Lee), GREG (Michel Stuart), CASSIE (Donna McKechn
JUDY (Patricia Garland), RICHIE (Ronald Dennis), AL (Don Percassi), KRIST

ILA (Carole Bishop), BOBBY (Thomas J. Walsh), BEBE (Nancy Lane),
nee Baughman), VAL (Pamela Blair) and MARK (Cameron Mason)

ALL:
> I'VE GOT TO GET THIS SHOW.

> (*While holding last chord on "show," the line walks downstage as the lights dim to black. Mirror panels change to black. The lights bump up revealing the line with their photos in front of their faces. The line is, stage right to stage left:* DON, MAGGIE, MIKE, CONNIE, GREG, CASSIE, SHEILA, BOBBY, BEBE, JUDY, RICHIE, AL, KRISTINE, VAL, MARK, PAUL *and* DIANA. LARRY *is down left, not part of the line*)

ZACH: Larry, collect the pictures and resumes, please.

> (LARRY *collects the pictures from stage left to right as the lights on the line dim leaving* PAUL *in a head spot*)

PAUL:
> WHO AM I ANYWAY?
> AM I MY RESUME?
> THAT IS A PICTURE OF A PERSON I DON'T KNOW.

> WHAT DOES HE WANT FROM ME?
> WHAT SHOULD I TRY TO BE?
> SO MANY FACES ALL AROUND, AND HERE WE GO.
> I NEED THIS JOB, OH GOD, I NEED THIS SHOW.

> (*Music out. Lights come up on the line*)

ZACH: Today, I want you to tell me your stage name, real name if it's different. And I'd also like to know where you were born and when.

SHEILA (*Stage whisper*): Terrific!

VAL (*Stage whisper*): Fabulous!

JUDY (*Raising her hand*): Ah . . . excuse me, sir . . . do we have to? I mean it's not very polite to ask a lady her age.

ZACH: Being polite doesn't interest me. Your age does. And I want to know your age. Okay, let's go down the line. We'll start on the end, stage right.

> (*The line looks to* DON; *he is talking to* MAGGIE, *who hits his leg, then he turns out to* ZACH)

DON: Ah . . . twenty-six.

ZACH: Start with your name and step forward.

DON (*Stepping forward*): My real name is Don Kerr. Ah—Kansas City, Kansas. October 20, 1949. (*Backs into line*)

ZACH: Next.

MAGGIE (*Stepping out*): Maggie Winslow.

ZACH: Louder.

MAGGIE: Maggie Winslow . . . sometimes known as Margaret, Margie, Peggy . . . all of the above. Whatever, it's real and I was born in San Mateo, California on a Thursday evening at 10:40 p.m., August 17, 1950. (*Backs into line*)

MIKE (*Stepping forward*): I'm Mike Costa—it used to be Costafalone. Born in Trenton, New Jersey, July 9, 1951, which makes me twenty-four. (*Backs to line*)

ZACH: Next.

CONNIE (*Coming forward*): Connie Wong. It's always been Connie Wong. I was born in Chinatown—Lower East Side. (*Steps back in line*)

MAGGIE (Kay Cole): "Maggie Winslow . . . sometimes known as Margaret, Margie, Peggy . . . all of the above."

ZACH: Your age?

BOBBY: Go on, Miss Wong.

CONNIE (*Stepping forward*): Ah . . . December 5, four thousand six hundred and forty-two. The Year of the Chicken. (*Backs to line*)

ZACH: Next.

GREG (*Coming forward*): My real name is Sidney Kenneth Beckenstein. My Jewish name is Rochmel Lev Ben Yokov Meyer Beckenstein, and my professional name is Gregory Gardner. Very East Side, and I do not deny it. Born August 2, 1943.

CASSIE (*Stepping out*): Cassie . . . Ah . . . Zach, could I talk to you for a minute?

ZACH: Sure, go ahead.

CASSIE: Well, I mean privately. (*She starts for steps to aisle*)

ZACH: Not right now, Cassie. I'm running about an hour behind.

CASSIE: Well, I know, but I . . .

ZACH: Next.

(CASSIE *goes back to line*)

SHEILA (*Stepping forward*): I'm Sheila Bryant. Really Sara Rosemary Bryant, which I really hate. I was born August 8, 1946 in Colorado Springs, Colorado. And I'm going to be thirty real soon. And I'm real glad. (*Backs into line*)

BOBBY (*Stepping downstage*): I'm Robert Charles Joseph Henry Mills

Photo by Martha Swope

GREG (Michel Stuart): "My real name is Sidney Kenneth Beckenstein . . . . My professional name is Gregory Gardner."

III, that's my real name too. I come from upstate New York near Buffalo, I can't remember the name of the town . . . I blocked it out. Born March 15, 1950. (*Back to line*)

BEBE (*Stepping forward*): My name is Bebe Benzenheimer . . . and I know, I gotta change it. Born June 6, 1949. I come from Boston, and here I am. (*Embarrassed, she backs into line*)

JUDY (*Coming forward*): My name is Judy Turner. My real name is Lana Turner. (*Laughing at her own joke*) No, no, no, no, no—it's always been Judy Turner. Born July 21, 1947. (*She starts backing up; RICHIE starts out, she stops him and goes on*) Oh, I was born in El Paso . . . El Paso, Texas. (*Backs into line*)

ZACH: Good. Next.

RICHIE (*Steps out of line*): My name is Richie Walters. I'm from Herculaneum, Missouri. I was born on a full moon on June 13, 1948. And I'm black.

AL: I'm Alan DeLuca. January 11, 1945. I come from the Bronx.

KRISTINE (*Taking a step forward*): I'm Kristine Urich, Kristine Evelyn Urich. Born September 1, 1953. (*Backs into line*)

AL (*To* KRISTINE): Tell him where you're from.

KRISTINE (*Takes a step forward*): Oh—I'm from St. Louis, Missouri. (*Goes back to line;* AL *prompts her*) Oh, and my married name is DeLuca.

(*They put their arms around each other and smile*)

ZACH: Oh, I didn't know, Al. Congratulations.

AL: Thanks.

ZACH: Next.

VAL (*Stepping forward*): Well, as far as I'm concerned I'm Valerie Clark. But my parents think I'm Margaret Mary Houlihan. (*To the group*) Couldn't you just die? I was born in the middle of nowhere. A little town called Arlington, Vermont. (*Stepping backwards*) Bye, bye.

ZACH: How old are you?

VAL: Old . . . No . . . twenty- . . . five.

MARK (*Loudly, coming forward*): Ah, Mark Anthony. Really Mark Philip Lawrence Tabori. Tempe, Arizona. I'm twenty. (*Backs into line*)

BOBBY (*To* SHEILA): Oh, Jesus.

MARK (*Stepping forward again*): And if I get this show, I'll work real hard. (*Backs up*)

SHEILA (*Under her breath*): Oh, brother.

VAL (*To* MARK): Don't let 'em bug you, honey.

PAUL: Paul San Marco. It's my stage name. My real name is Ephrain Ramirez. I was born in Spanish Harlem— October 22, 1947.

DIANA (*Stepping forward*): My name is Diana Morales. And I didn't change it 'cause I figured ethnic was in. Six-ten-forty-eight. You got that? And I was born on a Hollywood bed in the Bronx. (*She backs into line*)

ZACH: Go on, Diana.

DIANA (*Stepping out again*) Go on—what? (*Music under*) Oh, oh, you wanna know how tall I am? The color of my eyes? Or how many shows I've done? I just gave you my picture and resume, everything you wanna know is right there.

ZACH: I know. Now, tell me what's not on it.

DIANA: Like what?

ZACH: Talk about yourself.

DIANA: Talk about—what?

ZACH: Tell me about the Bronx.

DIANA: What's to tell about the Bronx? It's uptown and to the right.

ZACH: What did you do there?

DIANA: In the Bronx? Mostly wait to get out.

ZACH: What made you start dancing?

DIANA: Who knows? I have rhythm—I'm Puerto Rican. I always jumped around and danced. Hey, do you want to know if I can act? Gimme a scene to read, I'll act, I'll perform. But I can't just talk. Please, I'm too nervous.

ZACH: Then relax.

DIANA: Look, I really don't mind talking . . . but I just can't be the first . . . please.

ZACH (*With an edge*): You want this job, don't you?

DIANA: Sure I want the job.

(*Music fades out*)

ZACH: All right, Diana, back in line.

(DIANA *backs in line. During the following speech the lights dim, a spotlight moves from stage left to stage right and lights their faces one at a time in tempo—every four counts—with the music*)

ZACH: Before we do any more dancing—(*Music under*) and we will be dancing some more—let me explain something. I'm looking for a strong dancing chorus. I need people that look terrific together—and that can work together as a group. But there are some small parts that have to be played by the dancers I hire. Now, I have your pictures and resumes, I know what shows you've been in—but that's not gonna help me. And I don't want to give you just a few lines to read. I think it would be better if I knew something about you—about your personalities. So, I'm going to ask you some questions. I want to hear you talk. Treat it like an interview. I don't want you to think you have to perform. I just want to hear you talk and be yourselves. And everybody just relax—as much as you can.

(*Music fades out as lights up on the line.* SHEILA *raises her hand*)

Sheila?

SHEILA: How many people do you want?

ZACH: Four and four.

JUDY: Forty-four?

BEBE (*To* JUDY): No. Four *and* four.

ZACH: Four boys. Four girls.

SHEILA: Need any women?

ZACH: Okay, Mike, I'll start with you.

> (*Spotlight picks up* MIKE)

MIKE: Me? Don't you want to start at the end?

ZACH: No. I'll start with you—and relax.

MIKE: I could if you started at the end.

> (*Music under.* MIKE *slowly steps forward*)

What do you wanna know?

ZACH: What do you want to tell me?

MIKE: I'd like to tell you to start at the end. (*Fidgets*) Ah, I can't think of a thing.

ZACH: Yes you can. Why did you start dancing?

MIKE: Oh—because my sister did. I come from this big Italian family. My grandmother was always hanging out the window, leaning on a little pillow. 'Cause that's what Italian grandmothers do—hang out windows. I was the last of twelve . . . I was an accident. (*The group laughs*) I was. That's what my sister told me . . . Oh . . . That was the sister, Rosalie—She was the one who started taking dance lessons. My mother would take her every Saturday, she used to take me along. I liked going.

ZACH: How old were you?

Photo by Martha Swope

MIKE (Wayne Cilento): "I CAN DO THAT"

MIKE: Four. And I'd sit there all perky and . . .

>   (*Lights dim on line. He sings*)

I'M WATCHIN' SIS
GO PITTERPAT.
SAID,
"I CAN DO THAT,
I CAN DO THAT."

KNEW EV'RY STEP
RIGHT OFF THE BAT.
SAID,
"I CAN DO THAT,
I CAN DO THAT."

ONE MORNING SIS WON'T GO TO DANCE CLASS.
I GRAB HER SHOES AND TIGHTS AND ALL,
BUT MY FOOT'S TOO SMALL,
SO,

I STUFF HER SHOES
WITH EXTRA SOCKS,
RUN SEVEN BLOCKS
IN NOTHIN' FLAT.
HELL,
I CAN DO THAT,
I CAN DO THAT!
>   (*Dances*)
I GOT TO CLASS
AND HAD IT MADE
AND SO I STAYED
THE REST OF MY LIFE.
ALL THANKS TO SIS
(NOW MARRIED AND FAT),

I CAN DO THIS.
    (*Dances*)
THAT I CAN DO!
I CAN DO THAT.

    (*Lights back up on line. Speaking*)

And then everybody started calling me Twinkle-Toes.

    (*Music continues under*)

ZACH: Did that bother you?

MIKE: Naw, I figured let them say what they want.

ZACH: I don't buy that, Mike.

MIKE (*Shouting*): Well, sure it bothered me. I didn't want anybody calling me Twinkle-Toes just because I took a couple of dance lessons.

    (*Music fades out*)

ZACH: Okay, Mike—back in line.

    (*He obeys*)

Bobby, you're on.

BOBBY (*Stepping forward*): Well, actually, I don't . . . (*Music under*) know how I turned out as heavenly as I did. See, when I was five years old I was playing jacks—and the car fell down on my head.

    (*The group boos, groans, etc.*)

GREG: Get the hook.

ZACH: Bobby, are you gonna do a routine?

BOBBY: No, no . . . moving right along, moving along . . . Let's see . . . Do you wanna know about all the wonderful and exciting things that have happened to me in my life? Or do you want the truth?

ZACH: I'll take the truth.

BOBBY: Well, to begin with, I come from this quasi-middle-upper or upper-middle class, family-type-home. I could never figure out which but it was real boring. I mean, we had money—but no taste. You know the kind of house—Astroturf on the patio? Anyway, my mother had a lot of card parties and was one of the foremost bridge cheaters in America. My father worked for this big corporation. They used to send him out into the field a lot—to drink. Better that than to find him lying on his office floor . . . But he was okay . . . I was the strange one.

ZACH: How strange?

BOBBY: Real, real strange. I used to love to give garage recitals. BIZARRE recitals. This one time I was doing Frankenstein as a musicale and I spray-painted this kid silver—all over. They had to rush him to the hospital. 'Cause he had that thing when your pores can't breathe . . . (*Music under*) He lived 'cause luckily I didn't paint the soles of his feet and . . .

> (*Lights dim on line, except for specials on those singing, leaving* BOBBY *in a dimmed spot continuing his story in pantomime*)

RICHIE:
AND . . .
WHAT IF I'M NEXT?
WHAT IF I'M NEXT?
WHAT AM I GONNA DO?
I HAVEN'T A CLUE.
I GOTTA THINK OF SOMETHING.

BOBBY (Thomas J. Walsh): "You know the kind of house—Astroturf on the patio?"

WHAT DOES HE WANT?
WHAT DOES HE WANT?
STORIES FROM THE PAST?
I BETTER FIND ONE FAST!

MAGGIE, GREG, BEBE, RICHIE, VAL, PAUL (*Each in a special "thought" light*):
WHAT SHOULD I SAY?
WHAT CAN I TELL HIM?

(*Lights back up on line. Music continues under*)

BOBBY: As I got older I kept getting stranger and stranger. I used to go down to this busy intersection near my house at rush hour and direct traffic. I just wanted to see if anybody'd notice me. That's when I started breaking into people's houses—oh, I didn't steal anything—I'd just rearrange their furniture. And . . .

(*Again lights on line dim except for specials on those singing*)

VAL:
AND . . .
ORPHAN AT THREE.
ORPHAN AT THREE.
MOTHER AND DAD BOTH GONE.
RAISED BY A SWEET EX-CON.
TIED UP AND RAPED AT SEVEN.

SERIOUSLY!
SERIOUSLY!
NOTHING TOO OBSCENE!
I'D BETTER KEEP IT CLEAN!

DON, CONNIE, SHEILA, RICHIE, VAL, DIANA:
WHAT SHOULD I SAY?
WHAT CAN I TELL HIM?

(*Lights up on line. Music continues under*)

BOBBY: School? You wanna hear about school? I went to P. S. Shit . . . See, I was the kind of kid that was always getting slammed into lockers and stuff like that. Not only by the students—by the teachers too. Oh, and I hated sports, *hated* sports. And sports were very big. I mean, it was jock city, but I didn't make one team. See, I couldn't catch a ball if it had Elmer's Glue on it. And wouldn't my father have to be this big ex-football hero? He was so humiliated, he didn't know what to tell his friends. So he told 'em all I had polio. On Father's Day I used to limp for him. (*He demonstrates*) And . . .

(*Lights dim again leaving singers in specials*)

JUDY:
   AND . . .
   GOD, I'M A WRECK.
   GOD, I'M A WRECK.
   I DON'T KNOW WHERE TO START.
   I'M GONNA FALL APART.
   WHERE ARE MY CHILDHOOD MEM'RIES?

   WHO WERE THE BOYS?
   WHAT WERE MY TOYS?
   GONE BEYOND RECALL!
   AND WHY AM I SO TALL?!!

   WHAT SHOULD I SAY?

VAL, RICHIE, MAGGIE, CONNIE, JUDY, DIANA, MIKE:
   WHAT CAN I TELL HIM?

JUDY:
   AND . . .

CONNIE and MAGGIE:
   AND . . .

RICHIE:
   AND . . .

VAL and DIANA:
   AND . . .

   (*Lights back up on line. Music out*)

BOBBY: And my mother kept saying: "If you don't stop setting your brother on fire, we're going to have to send you away." And I was always thinking up these spectacular ways how to kill myself. But then I realized—to commit suicide in Buffalo is redundant.

ZACH: Okay, Bobby. Back in line.

   (BOBBY *steps back in line*)

   Sheila.

SHEILA (*Remaining in line*): Yeeees? You want me?

ZACH: Yes.

SHEILA (*To the group, but more to* BOBBY): He wants me.

ZACH: To talk.

   (*Music under*)

SHEILA (*Stepping forward*): Right. What do you want to know about me first?

ZACH: Try, ah, why are you in this business?

Photo by Martha Swope

SHEILA (Carole Bishop): "That light . . . what color is that? Do you have anything softer?"

SHEILA: Well . . . I wanted to be a prima ballerina. (*Grimacing at the spotlight*) That light . . . What color is that? Do you have anything softer?

ZACH: Don't worry about the lights . . . Just talk.

SHEILA: Well . . . Like I said, I wanted to be a ballerina. Because my mother was a ballerina—until my father made her give it up.

ZACH: Sheila, come downstage.

    (SHEILA *walks downstage seductively, one step*)

Closer.

SHEILA (*Walks further downstage*): Can I sit on your lap?

ZACH: Do you always come on like this?

SHEILA: No, sometimes I'm aggressive . . . Actually I'm a Leo . . .

ZACH: What's that supposed to mean?

SHEILA: It means the other eleven months of the year have to watch out . . . I'm very strong.

ZACH: Maybe too strong.

SHEILA: Am I doing something you don't like? I mean, you told me to be myself.

ZACH: Just bring it down.

SHEILA: Bring what down?

ZACH: Your attitude. Tell me about your parents.

SHEILA: My parents?

ZACH: Your father.

SHEILA: Him?

ZACH: Your mother.

SHEILA: My mother . . . My mother was raised like a little nun. She couldn't go out—she couldn't even babysit.

ZACH: Sheila, don't perform . . . Just talk.

SHEILA (*In monotone*): But she wanted to be a dancer and she had all these scholarships and all that. And when she got married, my father made her give it up . . . (*Breaking monotone, to the line*) . . . Isn't this exciting? And then she had this daughter—me—and she made her what *she* wanted to be. And she was fabulous the way she did it . . . Do you want to know how she did it?

ZACH: Yes . . . But first, your hair . . .

SHEILA: What? You don't like it.

ZACH: No . . . Let it down.

SHEILA (*Taking the pins out*): That's what I've been trying to do. (*She shakes her hair down*) Better . . . ?

ZACH: Better . . . Go on.

SHEILA: Oh, how she did it . . . Well, first, she took me to see all the ballets. And then, she gave me her old toe shoes—which I used to run down the sidewalk in—on my toes—at five. And then I saw *The Red Shoes*—

(*The girls on line respond*)

—and I wanted to be that lady, that redhead. And then, when she saw I really had to dance, she said: "You can't do it until you're eight." Well by then, I was only six . . . (*Music fades out*) and I said "BUT I'VE GOT TO DANCE." (*To the group*) I mean, anything to get out of the house.

ZACH: What?

SHEILA: Nothing.

ZACH: What did you say?

SHEILA: I just said that I wanted to get out of my house.

ZACH: Why?

SHEILA: The truth?

ZACH: Sure, you're strong enough.

(*Music under*)

SHEILA: Well . . . Let's face it . . . My family scene was—ah . . . not good!

(*Lights go out on line. They back up, turn, walk to back wall, facing upstage.* SHEILA *sings*)

DADDY ALWAYS THOUGHT THAT HE MARRIED BENEATH HIM.
THAT'S WHAT HE SAID, THAT'S WHAT HE SAID.
WHEN HE PROPOSED HE INFORMED MY MOTHER

HE WAS PROBABLY HER VERY LAST CHANCE.
AND THOUGH SHE WAS TWENTY-TWO,
THOUGH SHE WAS TWENTY-TWO,
THOUGH SHE WAS TWENTY-TWO,
SHE MARRIED HIM.

LIFE WITH MY DAD WASN'T EVER A PICNIC.
MORE LIKE A "COME AS YOU ARE."
WHEN I WAS FIVE I REMEMBER MY MOTHER
DUG EARRINGS OUT OF THE CAR.
I KNEW THAT THEY WEREN'T HERS, BUT IT WASN'T
SOMETHING YOU'D WANT TO DISCUSS.
HE WASN'T WARM.
WELL, NOT TO HER.
WELL, NOT TO US.

BUT
EVERYTHING WAS BEAUTIFUL AT THE BALLET.
GRACEFUL MEN LIFT LOVELY GIRLS IN WHITE.
YES,
EVERYTHING WAS BEAUTIFUL AT THE BALLET.
HEY!
I WAS HAPPY . . . AT THE BALLET.
     (Speaking)
   That's when I started class . . .

          (BEBE *turns, walks downstage, is picked up in spot, as* SHEILA
          sings)

     UP A STEEP AND VERY NARROW STAIRWAY.

SHEILA and BEBE:
     TO THE VOICE LIKE A METRONOME.
     UP A STEEP AND VERY NARROW STAIRWAY.

SHEILA:

  IT WASN'T PARADISE . . .

BEBE:

  IT WASN'T PARADISE . . .

SHEILA and BEBE:

  IT WASN'T PARADISE . . .

SHEILA:

  BUT IT WAS HOME.

     (BEBE *comes further downstage,* SHEILA *faces upstage*)

BEBE:

  MOTHER ALWAYS SAID I'D BE VERY ATTRACTIVE
  WHEN I GREW UP, WHEN I GREW UP.
  "DIFF'RENT," SHE SAID, "WITH A SPECIAL SOMETHING
  AND A VERY, VERY PERSONAL FLAIR."
  AND THOUGH I WAS EIGHT OR NINE,
  THOUGH I WAS EIGHT OR NINE,
  THOUGH I WAS EIGHT OR NINE,
  I HATED HER.

  NOW,

  "DIFF'RENT" IS NICE, BUT IT SURE ISN'T PRETTY.
  "PRETTY" IS WHAT IT'S ABOUT.
  I NEVER MET ANYONE WHO WAS "DIFF'RENT"
  WHO COULDN'T FIGURE THAT OUT.
  SO BEAUTIFUL I'D NEVER LIVE TO SEE.
  BUT IT WAS CLEAR,
  IF NOT TO HER,
  WELL, THEN . . . TO ME . . .
  THAT . . .

(MAGGIE *turns, walks downstage, is picked up by spot*)

MAGGIE and BEBE:
>EVERYONE IS BEAUTIFUL AT THE BALLET.
>EV'RY PRINCE HAS GOT TO HAVE HIS SWAN.
>YES,
>EV'RYONE IS BEAUTIFUL AT THE BALLET.

MAGGIE:
>HEY! . . .

BEBE:
>I WAS PRETTY . . .

SHEILA (*Turning front*):
>AT THE BALLET.

MAGGIE, SHEILA and BEBE (*As they sing, a group up right demonstrates a Barre*):
>UP A STEEP AND VERY NARROW STAIRWAY
>TO THE VOICE LIKE A METRONOME.
>UP A STEEP AND VERY NARROW STAIRWAY

MAGGIE:
>IT WASN'T PARADISE . . .

BEBE:
>IT WASN'T PARADISE . . .

SHEILA:
>IT WASN'T PARADISE . . .

MAGGIE, SHEILA and BEBE:
>BUT IT WAS HOME.

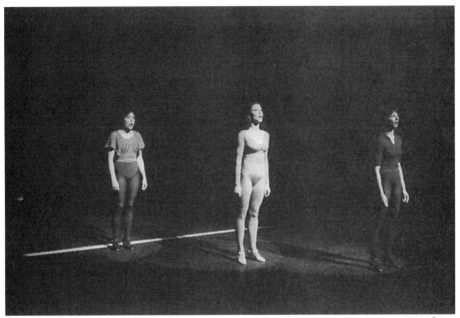

Photo by Martha Swope

MAGGIE (Kay Cole), SHEILA (Carole Bishop) and
BEBE (Nancy Lane): "AT THE BALLET"

(Spots dim on SHEILA *and* BEBE, *leaving* MAGGIE *in brightest spot. Group goes back to line. Music continues under)*

MAGGIE: I don't know what they were for or against really, except each other. I mean I was born to save their marriage but when my father came to pick my mother up at the hospital he said, "Well, I thought this was going to help. But I guess it's not . . . " Anyway, I did have a fantastic fantasy life. I used to dance around the living room with my arms up like this. My fantasy was that I was an Indian Chief . . . And he'd say to me, "Maggie, do you wanna dance?" And I'd say, "Daddy, I would love to dance."

(Other two girls sing backup syllables {do-do-do's} behind solo lines 'til MAGGIE'*s solo refrain)*

BEBE:
BUT IT WAS CLEAR . . .

SHEILA:
WHEN HE PROPOSED . . .

MAGGIE:
THAT I WAS BORN TO HELP THEIR MARRIAGE AND WHEN . . .

SHEILA:
THAT'S WHAT HE SAID . . .

BEBE:
THAT'S WHAT SHE SAID . . .

MAGGIE:
I USED TO DANCE AROUND THE LIVING ROOM . . .

SHEILA:
HE WASN'T WARM . . .

BEBE:
>NOT TO HER . . .

MAGGIE:
>I WAS AN INDIAN CHIEF AND HE'D SAY:
>"MAGGIE, DO YOU WANNA DANCE?"
>AND I'D SAY, "DADDY, I WOULD LOVE TO . . . "

>EV'RYTHING WAS BEAUTIFUL AT THE BALLET,
>RAISE YOUR ARMS, AND SOMEONE'S ALWAYS THERE.
>YES, EV'RYTHING WAS BEAUTIFUL AT THE BALLET,
>AT THE BALLET,
>AT THE BALLET!!!

>>*(Dance section, for which black panels turn to mirror panels)*

MAGGIE, BEBE and SHEILA:
>YES, EV'RYTHING WAS BEAUTIFUL AT THE BALLET.

MAGGIE:
>HEY! . . .

BEBE:
>I WAS PRETTY . . .

SHEILA:
>I WAS HAPPY . . .

MAGGIE:
>"I WOULD LOVE TO . . . "

MAGGIE, BEBE and SHEILA:
>AT . . . THE . . . BALLET.

>>*(The group is back on line, the mirror panels turn to black again. Music cadence and out)*

ZACH: Okay, Kristine.

KRISTINE: Oh, no—me?

AL: That's what he said.

KRISTINE (*Steps downstage*): Well, ah . . . Oh. God—I don't know where to begin.

AL: Tell him how you started.

(*Music under*)

KRISTINE: Oh—Ah, well, everybody says that when I was little every time they put on the radio, I'd just get up and start dancing. And, ah . . . Oh, this man came around to my house—selling . . . ah . . .

AL: Lessons.

KRISTINE: Oh, and he was a terrific salesman—I'll never forget it—he put me up against this television set—it was one of those great big square things—and then he turned me around, picked up my foot and touched it to the back of my head and said: "This little girl could be a star." Well, I don't know if it was the look on my face— or the fact that I wouldn't let go of his leg—But my mother saw how much it meant to me. I mean, I watched everything on television that had dancing on it—Especially—oh, God—every Sunday—it was, ah . . . ah . . .

AL: Ed Sullivan.

KRISTINE: Right—Ed Sullivan—every Sunday—like church. And, ah . . . oh, dear, what was I talking about? (*Backs to* AL)

AL: Ed Sullivan.

KRISTINE: No, no . . . It was—oh, right—Ed Sullivan. (*Steps back downstage*) I'm sorry. It's just—I'm really nervous.

ZACH: That's all right. Just take a minute and pull yourself together.

AL: (*Coming to her side*) For her—this is together.

KRISTINE: He's right. But anyway, I always knew what I wanted to do. I wanted to, like, be all those people in the movies. Only it's funny, I never wanted to be Ann Miller . . . I wanted to be—Doris Day. Except I had this little ah . . .

AL: Problem.

KRISTINE (*Sings*):
SEE I REALLY COULDN'T SING
I COULD NEVER REALLY SING

	AL (*Sings*):
WHAT I COULDN'T DO WAS . . .	. . . SING!
I HAVE TROUBLE WITH A . . .	. . . NOTE.
IT GOES ALL AROUND MY . . .	. . . THROAT.
IT'S A TERRIFYING . . .	. . . THING.
SEE, I REALLY COULDN'T HEAR	
WHICH NOTE WAS LOWER OR WAS . . .	. . . HIGHER.
WHICH IS WHY I DISAPPEAR	
IF SOMEONE SAYS, "LET'S START A . . .	. . . CHOIR."
HEY, WHEN I BEGIN TO . . .	. . . SHRIEK.
IT'S A CROSS BETWEEN A . . .	. . . SQUEAK.
AND A QUIVER OR A . . .	. . . MOAN.
IT'S A LITTLE LIKE A . . .	. . . CROAK.
OR THE RECORD PLAYER . . .	. . . BROKE.
WHAT IT DOESN'T HAVE IS . . .	. . . TONE.
OH, I KNOW YOU'RE THINKING	

AL (Don Percassi) and KRISTINE (Renee Baughman): "SING!"

WHAT A CRAZY . . .	. . . DINGALING.
BUT I REALLY COULDN'T . . .	. . . SING.
I COULD NEVER REALLY . . .	. . . SING.
WHAT I COULDN'T DO WAS . . .	. . . SING!

AL:
THREE BLIND MICE.

KRISTINE (*Off-key*):
THREE BLIND MICE . . .
    (*Speaking*)
It isn't intentional . . .

AL: She's doing her best,
    (*Sings*)
JINGLE BELLS, JINGLE BELLS . . .

KRISTINE:
JINGLE BELLS, JINGLE BELLS . . .
    (*Speaking*)
It really blows my mind . . .

AL: She gets depressed.

KRISTINE:

BUT WHAT I LACK IN PITCH I SURE	AL:
MAKE UP IN . . .	. . . POWER!
AND ALL MY FRIENDS SAY I AM	
PERFECT FOR THE	
(*Off-key*)	
SHOWER.	
STILL,	
I'M TERRIFIC AT A . . .	. . . DANCE.
GUYS ARE COMIN' IN THEIR . . .	. . . PANTS.

I'm a birdie on the . . .   . . . wing.
But when I begin to . . .   . . . chirp.
They say, "Who's the little . . .   . . . twerp
. . . Goin' 'pong' instead of . . .   . . . 'ping'?"
And when Christmas comes and
    all my friends go . . .

All:

Caroling,

Kristine: Al:
It is so dishearten . . .   . . . -ning.
It is so disquiet . . .   . . . -ting.
It is so discourag . . .   . . . -ging.
Darling, please stop answer . . .   . . . -ring!

See, I really couldn't . . .   . . . -sing.
I could never really . . .   . . . -sing.
What I couldn't do was . . .

All (*In parts with* Al *conducting the line and* Kristine):
Do, re, mi, fa, sol, la, ti, do
Do, ti, la, sol, fa, mi, re, do
La

Kristine (*Off-key*):
La . . .

All:
La

Kristine:
La . . .

GIRLS:

   Sing, sing

   Sing a sing a sing sing   BOYS:

   Sing, sing,   Never sing a note.

                                   Please never,

   Sing, sing,   Never sing a note,

                                   Don't ever . . .

KRISTINE (*Off-key*):

   . . . Sing.

ALL:

   Sing!

      (*Music out*)

ZACH: Okay, Al and Kristine, back in the line . . .

      (AL *and* KRISTINE *back into line*)

Mark . . .

MARK (*Comes downstage to the group*): Well, I get the feeling most of you always knew what you wanted to do. Me—I didn't. I was just a kid for a while. Oh, then one day—well—my father had this fabulous library in the back of the house—and when I was—about eleven, I guess—I found this medical textbook. It had pictures of the male and female anatomy. Well, I thought that was pretty interesting. I used to read that book a lot.

ZACH: Were you interested in medicine? Or were you just into the pictures?

MARK: No, I . . .

      (MARK *goes into pantomime. Lights dim and go out on line, leaving singers in specials*)

VAL:
>HELLO TWELVE,

RICHIE:
>HELLO THIRTEEN,

MAGGIE:
>HELLO LOVE.

AL:
>CHANGES, OH!

BEBE:
>DOWN BELOW.

DIANA:
>UP ABOVE.

VAL:
>TIME TO DOUBT,

MIKE:
>TO BREAK OUT,

RICHIE:
>IT'S A MESS,

MAGGIE:
>IT'S A MESS.

PAUL and JUDY:
>TIME TO GROW.

MAGGIE and AL:
>TIME TO GO

CONNIE, BOBBY and RICHIE:
>ADOLESCE,

ALL:
>ADOLESCE.
>TOO YOUNG TO TAKE OVER,
>TOO OLD TO IGNORE.

AL:
>GEE, I'M ALMOST READY,

ALL:
>BUT . . . WHAT . . . FOR?

>THERE'S A LOT
>I AM NOT
>CERTAIN OF.

>HELLO TWELVE,
>HELLO THIRTEEN,
>HELLO LOVE.

>*(Lights come up on group who are back on line)*

MARK (*Out of pantomime*): And from the book I diagnosed my own appendicitis. (*Sings*)
>NEXT DAY I WENT TO OUR DOCTOR DOWN THE BLOCK.
>SURE ENOUGH—ACUTE APPENDICITIS!
>THEY RUSHED ME RIGHT TO THE HOSPITAL.
>WELL, I FIGURED THIS BOOK
>WOULD COVER EV'RYTHING
>THE REST OF MY LIFE.

Photo by Martha Swope

MARK (Cameron Mason): "It was the only time the church helped me out."

(Speaking)
And when I was thirteen, I had my first . . . wet dream. I went right back to the book . . . Milky discharge . . . milky discharge, milky discharge . . . GONORRHEA! I was in shock, I mean . . . GONORRHEA! Before I'd even started. I was terrified. I couldn't tell my mother I had . . . GONORRHEA! So, the book said, drink a lot of water . . .

ZACH: Is that all the book said?

MARK: No, it said take penicillin, strepto-something-or-other, but I couldn't do anything about that unless I told somebody.
(Sings)
SO ALL I COULD DO WAS DRINK THE WATER,
AND I DRANK LIKE TWENTY GLASSES A DAY.
(Speaking)
For three weeks. I almost drowned. Finally I went to confession and told the priest that I had GONORRHEA! Well, he was in shock, too.
(Sings)
"WHO HAVE YOU BEEN WITH, MY SON?"
(Speaking)
Nobody. Nobody.
(Sings)
"THEN HOW CAN YOU HAVE . . . GONORRHEA?"
(Speaking)
I told him about the book's diagnosis for milky discharge and he set me straight. It's the only time the Church ever helped me out. Well, I was . . . *(He goes back to line)*

CONNIE *(Stepping forward and singing)*:
FOUR FOOT TEN.
FOUR FOOT TEN.
THAT'S THE STORY OF MY LIFE.

Photo by Martha Swope

CONNIE (Baayork Lee): "Four feet ten . . . That's the story of my life."

I REMEMBER WHEN EV'RY BODY WAS MY SIZE.
> (*Speaking*)

Boy, was that great. But then everybody started moving up and— there I was, stuck at . . .
> (*Sings*)
> FOUR FOOT TEN.
> FOUR FOOT TEN.
> (*Speaking*)

But I kept hoping and praying.
> (*Sings*)
> I USED TO HANG FROM A PARALLEL BAR BY THE HOUR,
> HOPING I'D STRETCH
> JUST AN INCH MORE.
> (*Speaking*)

'Cause I was into dancing then, and I was good. And I wanted so much to grow up to be a prima ballerina. Then I went out for . . . CHEERLEADER! And they told me: "No dice, you'll get lost on the football field. The pom-poms are bigger than you." I spent my whole childhood waiting to grow . . .

> (CONNIE *goes into pantomime. The others have moved to dance formation. Each solo is picked up by spotlight*)

VAL:
> TITS! WHEN AM I GONNA GROW TITS?

PAUL:
> SECRET, MY WHOLE LIFE WAS A SECRET.

MIKE: ONE LITTLE FART! . . . And they called me Stinky for three years. (*Screamed in frustration until start of vocal*) Aahhh!

ALL (*except* CONNIE):
> GOODBYE TWELVE,
> GOODBYE THIRTEEN,

HELLO LOVE . . .

BEBE:

ROBERT GOULET, ROBERT GOULET,
MY GOD, ROBERT GOULET!

ALL:

. . . OH!
DOWN BELOW,
UP ABOVE . . .

DON:

PLAYING DOCTOR WITH EVELYN.

ALL:

LA LA LA

RICHIE:

I'LL SHOW YOU MINE,

ALL:

LA LA

RICHIE:

YOU SHOW ME YOURS.

ALL:

LA LA

KRISTINE: Seeing Daddy . . . naked!

ALL:

TIME TO GROW,
TIME TO GO . . .

SHEILA: Surprise!

ALL:
LA LA LA

SHEILA: Mom and Dad were doing it.

BOBBY:
I'M GONNA BE A MOVIE STAR.

CONNIE (*Out of pantomime. The rest of the cast is now back on the line and lights come up*): But you see, the only thing about me that grew was my desire.
(*Sings*)
I WAS NEVER GONNA BE MARIA TALLCHIEF. I WAS JUST . . .
(*Speaking*)
This peanut on pointe! That was my whole trip—my size. It still is. God, my last show I was thirty-two and I played a fourteen-year-old brat . . .

ZACH: An hah, the Year of the Chicken, thirty-two?

RICHIE (*Imitating a chicken*): Puck-puck-puck-puck, girl!

CONNIE: So, I got caught . . . But I don't look it. And I shouldn't knock it 'cause I've always been able to work . . .
(*Sings*)
FROM THE TIME I WAS FIVE IN KING AND I.
KING AND I.
UP 'TIL NOW I'VE NEVER STOPPED
'CAUSE WHATEVER I AM
I AM . . .

(CONNIE *backs to her position in line and* DIANA *runs to center*)

DIANA: . . . So excited because I'm gonna go to the High School of Performing Arts! I mean, I was dying to be a serious actress. Anyway, it's the first day of acting class—and we're in the auditorium and the teacher, Mr. Karp . . . Oh, Mr. Karp . . . Anyway, he puts us up on the stage with our legs around each other, one in back of the other and he says: "Okay . . . we're going to do improvisations. Now, you're on a bobsled. It's snowing out. And it's cold . . . Okay . . . GO!"

(The line people back up, run offstage left. DIANA sings)

EV'RY DAY FOR A WEEK WE WOULD TRY TO
FEEL THE MOTION, FEEL THE MOTION,
DOWN THE HILL.

EV'RY DAY FOR A WEEK WE WOULD TRY TO
HEAR THE WIND RUSH, HEAR THE WIND RUSH,
FEEL THE CHILL.

AND I DUG RIGHT DOWN TO THE BOTTOM OF MY SOUL
TO SEE WHAT I HAD INSIDE.
YES, I DUG RIGHT DOWN TO THE BOTTOM OF MY SOUL
AND I TRIED, I TRIED.
    (Speaking)
And everybody is going "Whooooshhh, whooooshhh . . . I feel the snow . . . I feel the cold . . . I feel the air." And Mr. Karp turns to me and he says, "Okay, Morales. What did you feel?"
    (Sings)
AND I SAID . . . "NOTHING,
I'M FEELING NOTHING."
AND HE SAYS "NOTHING
COULD GET A GIRL TRANSFERRED."

THEY ALL FELT SOMETHING,
BUT I FELT NOTHING

EXCEPT THE FEELING
THAT THIS BULLSHIT WAS ABSURD.
  (*Speaking*)
But I said to myself, "Hey, it's only the first week. Maybe it's genetic. They don't have bobsleds in San Juan."
  (*Sings*)
SECOND WEEK, MORE ADVANCED AND WE HAD TO
BE A TABLE, BE A SPORTS CAR . . .
ICE-CREAM CONE.

MR. KARP, HE WOULD SAY, "VERY GOOD, EX-
CEPT MORALES. TRY, MORALES,
ALL ALONE."

SO I DUG RIGHT DOWN TO THE BOTTOM OF MY SOUL
TO SEE HOW AN ICE-CREAM FELT.
YES, I DUG RIGHT DOWN TO THE BOTTOM OF MY SOUL
AND I TRIED TO MELT.

THE KIDS YELLED "NOTHING!"
THEY CALLED ME "NOTHING!"
AND KARP ALLOWED IT,
WHICH REALLY MAKES ME BURN.

THEY WERE SO HELPFUL.
THEY CALLED ME HOPELESS.
UNTIL I REALLY DIDN'T KNOW
WHERE ELSE TO TURN.
  (*Speaking*)
And Karp kept saying, "Morales, I think you should transfer to Girls' High. You'll never be an actress. Never!" *Jesus Christ!*
  (*Sings*)
WENT TO CHURCH, PRAYING, "SANTA MARIA,
SEND ME GUIDANCE, SEND ME GUIDANCE,"

Photo by Martha Swope

DIANE (Priscilla Lopez): "This man is nothing!"

On my knees.

Went to church, praying, "Santa Maria,
Help me feel it, help me feel it.
Pretty please!"

And a voice from down at the bottom of my soul
Came up to the top of my head.
And the voice from down at the bottom of my soul,
Here is what it said:

"This man is nothing!
This course is nothing!
If you want something,
Go find a better class.

And when you find one
You'll be an actress."
And I assure you that's what
Fin'lly came to pass.

Six months later I heard that Karp had died.
And I dug right down to the bottom of my soul . . . .
And cried,
'Cause I felt . . . nothing.
   (*Speaking*)
I mean, I didn't want him to die or anything, but . . .

   (*Music under as* DIANA *backs up, exits stage left.* DON *enters upstage right, crosses down below line*)

DON: The summer I turned fifteen, I lied about my age so I could join AGVA—you know . . .
   (*Sings*)
The night club union,

'Cause I could make sixty dollars a week
Working these strip joints
Outside of Kansas City.
I worked this one club for about eight weeks straight
And I really became friendly with this stripper.
    (*Speaking*)
Her name was Lola Latores and her dynamic, twin forty-fours.
Well, she really took to me. I mean, we did share the *only* dressing
room, and she did a lot of dressing . . .
    (*Sings*)
Anyway, she used to come and pick me up
And drive me to work nights.
Well, the neighbors would all be hanging outside
Of their windows,
And she'd drive up in her big pink Cadillac convertible
And . . . smile.
    (*Speaking*)
And I'd come tripping out of the house in my little tuxedo and my
tap shoes in my hand and we'd drive off down the block with her
long, flaming red hair just blowing in the wind.

    (DON *goes into pantomime and the other line people enter stage left.*
    Each soloist is picked up in head spot as they sing their lines)

ALL:

GOODBYE TWELVE,
GOODBYE THIRTEEN,
HELLO LOVE.

MAGGIE:

WHY DO I PAY FOR ALL THOSE LESSONS?
DANCE FOR GRAN'MA! DANCE FOR GRAN'MA!

    (*Chorus sings backup syllables under solo lines*)

DON (Ron Kuhlman): "And she'd drive up in her big pink Cadillac and . . . smile."

Photo by Martha Swope

BEBE:

> MY GOD, THAT STEVE MCQUEEN'S REAL SEXY,
> BOB GOULET OUT,
> STEVE MCQUEEN IN!

CASSIE:

> YOU CANNOT GO TO THE MOVIES
> UNTIL YOU FINISH YOUR HOMEWORK.

AL:

> WASH THE CAR,

MIKE:

> STOP PICKIN' YOUR NOSE.

MAGGIE:

> OH, DARLING, YOU'RE NOT OLD ENOUGH TO WEAR A BRA.
> YOU'VE GOT NOTHING TO HOLD IT UP.

MARK:

> LOCKED IN THE BATHROOM WITH *PEYTON PLACE*.
>
> (*Chorus out*)

VAL:

> TITS! WHEN AM I GONNA GROW TITS?

BOBBY:

> IF TROY DONAHUE COULD BE A MOVIE STAR,
> THEN I COULD BE A MOVIE STAR.
>
> (*The others are now upstage right;* BOBBY *joins them. They face upstage*)

DON: (*Out of pantomime*) Well, when the guys on the block saw Lola, they all wanted to know what the story was, and I told them about this big hot romance we were having, but actually she was going with this . . .

(DON *steps upstage into darkness and joins group and* JUDY *moves forward from upstage left*)

JUDY (*Sings*):
LITTLE BRAT!
THAT'S WHAT MY SISTER WAS . . .
A LITTLE BRAT.
AND THAT'S WHY I SHAVED HER HEAD.
I'M GLAD I SHAVED HER HEAD.
BUT THEN MY FATHER LOST HIS JOB
SO WE HAD TO LEAVE EL PASO
AND WE WOUND UP IN ST. LOUIE, MISSOURI.
WELL, IT WAS THE FURTHEST THING
FROM MY MIND
TO BE A DANCER,
BUT MY MOTHER WOULD EMBARRASS ME
SO WHEN SHE'D COME TO PICK ME UP
AT SCHOOL WITH ALL THOSE GREAT, BIG, YELLOW ROLLERS IN HER HAIR
NO MATTER HOW MUCH I BEGGED HER
AND SHE'D SAY:
(*Speaking*)
"What are you, ashamed of your own mother?"
(*Sings*)
BUT THE THING THAT MADE MY DADDY LAUGH SO MUCH
WAS WHEN I USED TO JUMP AND DANCE AROUND THE LIVING ROOM. . .

(JUDY *goes into pantomime. The people who sing "Mother" have moved into formation with* MAGGIE *center*)

MAGGIE:
PLEASE TAKE THIS MESSAGE
TO MOTHER FROM ME.

Carry it with you
Across the blue sea.
"Mother, oh, Mother,
Wherever I go
Your Maggie is missin' you so."

"Mother, oh, Mother
Wherever I go
Your Maggie is missin' you so."

AL:

Dad would take Mom to Roseland.
She'd come home with her shoes in her hand.

DIANA:

Mama fat,
Always in the kitchen cooking all the time.

SHEILA:

Darling, I can tell you now,
Your father went through life with an open fly.

VAL:

Tits! Where are my tits?

CASSIE:

Listen to your mother.
Those stage and movie people got there
Because they're special.

GREG:

You take after your father's side of the family,
The ugly side.

PAUL:

    Wait until your father gets home.

DON:

    Swear to God and hope to die.

    (*Lights fade on group; they join others to reform line facing upstage*)

JUDY (*Out of pantomime*):

    And it was the . . .
    First time I'd ever
    Seen a dead body.
    But then when I was fifteen
    The most terrible thing happened.
    The Ted Mack Amateur Hour held auditions in St. Louie
    And I didn't hear about it 'til after they'd gone
    And I nearly killed myself.
    (*Line turns and walks downstage*)
    Nearly killed myself.
    I tried to walk in front of a speeding streetcar
    And I remember noticing boys for the first time.
    (*Line people are now on line and lights come up. Speaking*)
Anyway, I remember practicing kissing with Leslie. She was my best girl friend. Did any of you ever practice kissing with another girl . . .
    (*Sings*)
So that when the time came you'd know how to?
    (*Listens, then speaks*)
No? . . . Oh my God.

    (*After a moment*)

KRISTINE: Judy?

JUDY: Did you, girl?

JUDY (Patricia Garland): "Did any of you ever practice kissing with another girl?"

KRISTINE: Yeah . . . but just a *couple* of times.

SHEILA: Oh, count me in.

JUDY: Thank God! (*Backing into line*) Anyway, I do remember . . .

GREG (*Stepping forward*): The worst thing in school was every time the teacher called on me . . .
    (*Sings*)
  I'D BE HARD, I'D BE HARD.
    (*Speaking*)
Really, I'd have to lean up against the desk like this. (*He demonstrates*) And the teacher would say:
    (*Sings*)
  "STAND UP STRAIGHT!"
    (*Speaking*)
"I can't, I have a pain in my side."
    (*Sings*)
  "STAND UP STRAIGHT."
    (*Speaking*)
Or walking down the hall, you'd have to walk like this,
    (*Sings*)
  WITH ALL YOUR BOOKS STACKED UP IN FRONT OF YOU.

MIKE: Yeah, I thought it was only me. I thought I was a sex maniac.

CONNIE and MAGGIE (*Sing*):
  YOU ARE!

BOBBY: I did too. I mean, it didn't go down for three years.

GREG: And the bus, the bus was the worst. I'd just look at a bus and . . .
    (*Sings*)
  BINGO!

(*Speaking*)

And then there was the time I was making out in the back seat with Sally Ketchum . . . We were necking and I was feeling her boobs and after about an hour or so she said . . .

(*Sings*)

"OOOHHHH! DON'T YOU WANT TO FEEL ANYTHING ELSE?"

(*Speaking*)

And I suddenly thought to myself: "No, I don't."

ZACH: Did that come as a surprise to you?

GREG: I guess, yeah. It was probably the first time I realized I was homosexual and I got so depressed because I thought being gay meant being a bum all the rest of my life and I said:

(*Sings*)

"GEE, I'LL NEVER GET TO WEAR NICE CLOTHES . . . "

(*Speaking*)

And I was really into clothes, I had this pair of powder blue and pink gabardine pants . . . "

(GREG *goes into pantomime, the group breaks upstage from the line*)

CHORUS:

GOODBYE TWELVE
GOODBYE THIRTEEN
HELLO LA-A-A-OVE.

AL:

EARLY TO BED,
EARLY TO RISE.
YOUR BROAD GOES OUT WITH
        OTHER GUYS.

CASSIE:

A DIAPHRAGM, A DIAPHRAGM.
I THOUGHT A DIAPHRAGM WAS UP
        HERE,
WHERE YOU BREATHE.

DON:
> I bought a car.
> I bought my first car.

MIKE (*Speaking*): Padiddle.

CHORUS:
> Changes, oh,
> Down below.
> Up a- . . .

MARK:
> Ev'ry girl I know has lockjaw of
> the legs.

CONNIE:
> You're not leaving this house
> 'til you're
> Twenty-one.

KRISTINE:
> The ugliest boy asked me to the
> prom,
> I stayed home.

MAGGIE:
> Life is an ashtray.

VAL:
> Shit.
> Made it through high school
> without
> Growing tits.

CHORUS:
> . . . Doubt,
> To break out
> It's a mess.

RICHIE:
> My trouble is wine, women and
> song.
> I can't get any of 'em.

TIME TO GROW,
TIME TO GO,
A-DO . . .

MIKE:
  YOUR BROTHER'S GOING TO MED-
    ICAL SCHOOL,
  AND YOU'RE DROPPING OUT TO BE A
    CHORUS BOY.
  NOTHING!

BEBE:
  STEVE MCQUEEN OUT.
  NUREYEV IN!

DIANA:
  YOU GOTTA KNOW SOMEBODY TO BE
    SOMEBODY.

MAGGIE:
  GRA—DU—A—TION!

SHEILA:
  ALL YOU RUN AROUND WITH ARE
    BUMS.

AL:
  I GOT NANCY'S PICTURE, ANNABELLE'S
    LOCKET,
  CYNTHIA'S RING AND LUCY'S PANTS.
  HEAD-ON COLLISION!
  EDDIE GOT KILLED . . .

RICHIE:
  LET'S DANCE, LET'S DANCE.

PAUL:
WHAT AM I GONNA SAY WHEN HE CALLS ON ME?

(Offstage singers fill in all voices, lyrics sung in counterpoint-stretto to lyric unison below)

JUDY:
MY ONLY ADOLESCENCE, MY ONLY ADOLESCENCE,
MY ONLY ADOLESCENCE.

JUDY and KRISTINE:
MY ONLY ADOLESCENCE.

KRISTINE:
MY ONLY ADOLESCENCE . . .

DIANA and BEBE:
WHERE DID IT GO? IT WAS SO . . .
WHERE DID IT GO? IT WAS SO . . .

VAL, DIANA and BEBE:
WHERE DID IT GO? IT WAS SO . . .
WHERE DID IT GO? IT WAS SO . . .

GREG, BOBBY and MIKE:
FRESHMAN, SOPHOMORE, JUNIOR, SENIOR,
FRESHMAN, SOPHOMORE, JUNIOR, SENIOR.

SHEILA, MAGGIE and DON:
THIRTEEN, FOURTEEN, FIFTEEN, SIXTEEN,
THIRTEEN, FOURTEEN, FIFTEEN, SIXTEEN.

MARK, CONNIE, CASSIE, RICHIE, MAGGIE, JUDY, PAUL, LARRY and AL:
SUDDENLY I'M SEVENTEEN AND

(Upstage black panels have changed to mirrors)

ALL:
SUDDENLY I'M SEVENTEEN AND . . .

SUDDENLY I'M SEVENTEEN AND . . .
SUDDENLY,

THERE'S A LOT
I AM NOT
CERTAIN OF,

GOODBYE TWELVE,
GOODBYE THIRTEEN,
HELLO . . .

> (*All form into four groups for "scat" counterpoint section and dance break*)

GIRLS:

DOO,
DIT DIT DOO, DIT DIT DOO, DIT DIT DOO, DIT DIT DOO,
DIT DIT DOO, DIT DIT DOO, DIT DIT DOO, DIT DIT DOO,
DIT DIT DOO, DIT DIT DOO, DIT DIT DOO, DIT DIT DOO,
DIT DIT DOO, DIT DIT DOO, DIT DIT DOO, DIT DIT DOO,

GIRLS:

DEE DU DEE DU DEE DU, DEE DEE DU DIT,
DEE DU DEE DU DEE DU, DEE DEE DU DIT,
DEE DU DEE DU DEE DU, DEE DEE DU DIT,
DEE DU DEE DU DEE DU, DEE DEE DU DIT,
DEE DU DEE DU DEE DU, DEE DEE DU DIT,
DEE DU DEE DU DEE DU, DEE DEE DU DIT,
DEE DU DEE DU DEE DU, DEE DEE DU DIT,
DEE DU DEE DU DEE DU, DEE DEE DU.

BOYS:

WAH, WAH WAH WAH, WAH, WAH WAH WAH,
WAH, WAH WAH WAH, WAH, WAH WAH WAH,
WAH, WAH WAH WAH, WAH, WAH WAH WAH,

RICHIE (Ronald Dennis): "Gimme the ball. Yeah!"

WAH, WAH WAH WAH, WAH.

BOYS:

    DOO, DOO DOO DOO DOO, DOO DOO DOO AH,
    DOO, DOO DOO DOO DOO, DOO DOO DOO AH,
    DOO, DOO DOO DOO DOO, DOO DOO DOO AH,
    DOO, DOO DOO DOO DOO, DOO DOO DOO AH,
    DOO, DOO DOO DOO DOO, DOO DOO DOO AH,
    DOO, DOO DOO DOO DOO, DOO DOO DOO AH,
    DOO, DOO DOO DOO DOO, DOO DOO DOO AH,
    DOO, DOO DOO DOO DOO, DOO DOO DOO AH,

> *(Dance breaks. The cast ends up in a clump center stage. Suddenly they break into an angry and animated montage of individual stories, then separate into two groups, right and left. RICHIE, left center stage, sings)*

RICHIE:

    GIMME THE BALL,
    GIMME THE BALL,
    GIMME THE BALL. YEAH!

    GIMME THE BALL,
    GIMME THE BALL,
    GIMME THE BALL. YEAH!

    I WAS ALWAYS RUNNIN' AROUND SHOUTIN',
    "GIMME THE BALL,
    GIMME THE BALL,
    GIMME THE BALL. YEAH!"

    I WAS SO ENTHUSIASTIC.
    I WAS IN EV'RYTHING.
    THE YEARBOOK IS FILLED WITH MY PICTURES,
    AND I WAS LUCKY 'CAUSE I GOT

A SCHOLARSHIP TO COLLEGE.
A SCHOLARSHIP TO COLLEGE!
SO I WENT.

ALL (*Chorus plus offstage singers*):
SO HE WENT.

RICHIE:
YES, I WENT.

ALL:
YES, HE WENT.

RICHIE:
SO I'M GONNA BE THIS KINDERGARTEN TEACHER . . .
(*Speaking*)
Imagine me—this kindergarten teacher? And I thought . . .
(*Sings*)
SHIT.

ALL:
SHIT, RICHIE.

RICHIE:
SHIT.

ALL:
SHIT, RICHIE.

RICHIE:	ALL:
WHAT ARE YOU GONNA BE?	SHIT, RICHIE, SHIT, RICHIE.
WHEN YOU GET SHOVED	SHIT, RICHIE, SHIT, RICHIE.
OUTTA HERE,	
HONEY, AIN'T NOBODY	SHIT, RICHIE, SHIT, RICHIE.

GONNA BE STANDIN' THERE
WITH NO SCHOLARSHIP TO LIFE.   SHIT, RICHIE, SHIT, RICHIE.

RICHIE:

AND I WAS SCARED.

ALL:

SHIT, RICHIE.

RICHIE:

SCARED.

ALL:

SHIT, RICHIE.

RICHIE:

SCARED!!

ALL:

SHIT, RICHIE.

RICHIE:

SCARED!!!

ALL:

SHIT, RICHIE.

(Chorus, plus offstage voices through end of the number)

GIRLS:

MY BRACES GONE.

BOYS:

MY PIMPLES GONE.

ALL:

> MY CHILDHOOD GONE,
> GOODBYE.

> GOODBYE TWELVE.
> GOODBYE THIRTEEN.
> GOODBYE FOURTEEN.
> GOODBYE FIFTEEN.
> GOODBYE SIXTEEN.
> GOODBYE SEVENTEEN.
> HELLO LOVE.

> GO TO IT.
> GO TO IT.
> GO TO IT.
> GO TO IT.
> GO TO IT.
> GO TO IT.

BOYS:

> AND NOW LIFE REALLY BEGINS.

GIRLS:

> GO TO IT.

BOYS:

> AND NOW LIFE REALLY BEGINS.

GIRLS:

> GO TO IT.

BOYS:

> AND NOW LIFE REALLY BEGINS.

GIRLS:

GO TO IT.

BOYS:

AND NOW LIFE REALLY BEGINS.

GIRLS:

GO TO IT.

ALL:

GO TO IT.

> (*Music out; mirrors to black. The company is back on line.* LARRY *is seated on* ZACH's *stool down right*)

VAL (*Stepping forward*): So, the day after I turned eighteen, I kissed the folks goodbye—got on a Trailways bus—and headed for the big bad apple. (*Music under*) June Allyson, right? 'Cause I wanted to be a Rockette. Oh, yeah, let's get one thing straight. See, I never heard about *The Red Shoes*, I never saw *The Red Shoes*, I didn't give a fuck about *The Red Shoes*. I decided to be a Rockette because this girl in my home town—Louella Heiner—had actually gotten out and made it to New York. And she was a Rockette. Well, she came home one Christmas to visit, and they gave her a parade. A goddam parade. I twirled a friggin' baton for two hours in the rain. Unfortunately, though, she got knocked up over Christmas— Merry Christmas—and never made it back to Radio City. That was my plan. New York, New York, here I come. Except I had one minor problem. See, I was ugly as sin! I was ugly, skinny, homely, unattractive and flat as a pancake. Get the picture? Anyway, I got off this bus in my little white shoes, my little white tights, my little white dress, my little ugly face, and my long blond hair— which was natural then. I looked like a fuckin' nurse! I had eighty- seven dollars in my pocket, and seven years of tap and acrobatics. I could do a hundred and eighty degree split and come up tapping the Morse Code. Well, with that kind of talent I figured the mayor would be waiting for me at Port Authority. Wrong! I had to wait six months for an audition. Well, finally the big day came. I showed up at the Music Hall with my red patent leather tap shoes. And I did my little tap routine. And this man said to me, "Can you do fankicks?" Well, sure I could do terrific fankicks. But they weren't good enough. Of course, what he was trying to tell me was . . . it was the way I looked, not the fankicks. So I said, "Fuck you, Radio City and the Rockettes, I'm gonna dance on Broadway." Well, Broadway—same story. Every audition. I mean I'd dance rings around girls and find myself in the alley with the other rejects. But, after a while I caught on. I mean, I had eyes . . . (*Looks to* SHEILA) I saw what they were hiring. I also swiped my dance card once—after an audition. And on a scale of ten . . . They gave me: for dance, ten. For looks, three. Well . . . (*Sings*)

DANCE: TEN; LOOKS: THREE.
AND I'M STILL ON UNEMPLOYMENT,
DANCING FOR MY OWN ENJOYMENT.
THAT AIN'T IT, KID. THAT AIN'T IT, KID.

"DANCE: TEN; LOOKS: THREE,"
IS LIKE TO DIE!
LEFT THE THEATRE AND
CALLED THE DOCTOR FOR
MY APPOINTMENT TO BUY . . .

TITS AND ASS.
BOUGHT MYSELF A FANCY PAIR.
TIGHTENED UP THE DERRIERE.
DID THE NOSE WITH IT.
ALL THAT GOES WITH IT.

TITS AND ASS!
HAD THE BINGO-BONGOS DONE.

VAL (Pamela Blair): "DANCE: TEN; LOOKS: THREE"

SUDDENLY I'M GETTING NASH'NAL TOURS!
TITS AND ASS WON'T GET YOU JOBS
UNLESS THEY'RE YOURS.

DIDN'T COST A FORTUNE NEITHER.
DIDN'T HURT MY SEX LIFE EITHER.

FLAT AND SASSY,
I WOULD GET THE STRAYS AND LOSERS.
BEGGARS REALLY CAN'T BE CHOOSERS.
THAT AIN'T IT, KID. THAT AIN'T IT, KID.

FIXED THE CHASSIS.
"HOW DO YOU DO!"
LIFE TURNED INTO AN
ENDLESS MEDLEY OF
"GEE, IT HAD TO BE YOU!"
WHY?

TITS AND ASS!
WHERE THE CUPBOARD ONCE WAS BARE,
NOW YOU KNOCK AND SOMEONE'S THERE.
YOU HAVE GOT 'EM, HEY.
TOP TO BOTTOM, HEY.

IT'S A GAS!
JUST A DASH OF SILICONE.
SHAKE YOUR NEW MARACAS AND YOU'RE FINE!
TITS AND ASS CAN CHANGE YOUR LIFE.
THEY SURE CHANGED MINE.
        (*Short dance cross, then* VAL *speaks*)
You're all looking at my tits now, aren't you?

SHEILA: They aren't very big.

VAL: I heard that, you bitch. I didn't want 'em like yours . . . I wanted them in proportion.

SHEILA: Well, you got what you paid for.

CONNIE: I wouldn't mind having just one of yours.

VAL: Well, go out and buy 'em. (*Sings*)
    HAVE IT ALL DONE.
    HONEY, TAKE MY WORD.
    GRAB A CAB, C'MON.
    SEE THE WIZARD ON
    PARK AND SEVENTY-THIRD
    FOR

    TITS AND ASS.
    ORCHESTRA AND BALCONY.
    WHAT THEY WANT IS WHATCHA SEE.
    KEEP THE BEST OF YOU.
    DO THE REST OF YOU.

    PITS OR CLASS.
    I HAVE NEVER SEEN IT FAIL.
    DEBUTANTE OR CHORUS GIRL OR WIFE.

    TITS AND ASS,
    YES, TITS AND ASS
    HAVE CHANGED . . .
    MY . . .
    LIFE . . . !

      (*Music out.* VAL *goes back to her place on line*)

ZACH: Paul . . .

      (*Music under*)

PAUL: Ah, sir.

ZACH: Would you step out of line?

> (PAUL *steps forward hesitantly. He waits, then . . .*)

When did you start dancing, Paul?

PAUL: Not until very late . . .

ZACH: Why?

PAUL: I don't know why . . . I just didn't . . .

ZACH: Well, what did you do?

PAUL: Oh . . . Nothing much . . .

> (*Underscoring music plays out under following dialogue*)

ZACH: Come on, Paul—you must have done something. How old were you when you did start dancing?

PAUL: Sixteen . . .

ZACH: Well—What did you do up until the time you were sixteen? I mean, what was your family like?

PAUL: We were close . . .

ZACH: Close . . . Brothers, sisters?

PAUL: Ah . . . Two sisters. One died when I was fourteen.

ZACH: How?

> (*The group reacts to this question*)

PAUL: I, ah . . . I really don't want to talk about that. I mean . . . Why do I have to talk about that?

CONNIE: Larry, can we please sit down?

LARRY (*Rises, crosses in. To* ZACH): Zach, can the kids sit down now?

SHEILA: And smoke? Can the adults please smoke?

ZACH: Alright, everybody take a break—out in the hall.

> (*Everyone collects their dance bags and exits slowly up right*)

Paul, we'll try this again later. Cassie . . . stay on stage, please.

> (*Music under and continuous under dialogue, through vocal and* CASSIE's *big dance*)

CASSIE (*Slowly walks center stage*): Well, this audition is really interesting, isn't it?

ZACH: Yeah . . . What are you doing here?

CASSIE: What do you think? . . . I need a job.

ZACH: In the chorus?

CASSIE: Oh, look, Zach, I'd love a part, of course, but I'll take what I can get.

ZACH: You're too good for the chorus, Cassie.

CASSIE: Too good? I did a couple of dance parts, so what?

ZACH: You were featured, you stopped two shows cold, your career was going fine here in New York.

CASSIE: I can't get a job, Zach . . . God, you sound like all my friends—my fans. Acting like I'm a star and don't know it—when the truth is I never even came close and nobody has the guts to tell me. Well, it would be nice to be a star . . . But I'm not, I'm a dancer. (*Lights go out, leaving her head in spot and special. She sings*)
GIVE ME SOMEBODY TO DANCE FOR,
GIVE ME SOMEBODY TO SHOW.
LET ME WAKE UP IN THE MORNING TO FIND
I HAVE SOMEWHERE EXCITING TO GO.

(*Lights come back up*)

ZACH: So, you're going through a slow period, it happens to everyone. Something will happen.

CASSIE: That's what I kept telling myself in California, and I kept telling myself that and telling myself that . . . Well, nothing will happen. I can't act.

ZACH: What?

CASSIE: I can't act. And there I am in California supposed to be this actress. Well, it didn't take me very long to find out I can't act . . . Didn't take Hollywood very long either.

ZACH: You didn't work out there?

CASSIE: Oh, sure . . . A rotten part in a so-so film—part ended up getting cut, thank God—I was a go-go dancer in a TV movie of the week. Let's see—Oh, yeah—commercials, I almost got to squeeze a roll of toilet paper but I lost out in the finals. Isn't that something? Seventeen years in the business and I end up flunking toilet paper squeezing? And I was a dancing Band-Aid—that was fun . . . We had an earthquake . . . And I got a terrific tan—and surely you must have heard about . . .

ZACH: I did hear you were going out with some big agent. Being a bit wild, running around, carrying on . . .

CASSIE: Well, when you're a woman of leisure, what else is there to do but get a bit wild and run around? Not to mention getting fat—and going crazy—Which is why I came back to New York and which is why I am here today, Zach, old dear . . . Little pussy cat. I need a job. (*Lights go out as on last vocal. She sings*)
TO HAVE SOMETHING THAT I CAN BELIEVE IN.
TO HAVE SOMETHING TO BE.
USE ME . . . CHOOSE ME.

    (*Lights back up*)

ZACH: I just can't see you dancing in the chorus, Cassie.

CASSIE: Why not?

ZACH: Listen, if you need some money, call my business manager.

CASSIE: Well, sure I need money. Who doesn't? But I don't need a handout. I need a job. I need a job and I don't know any other way to say it. Do you want me to say it again?

ZACH: No.

CASSIE: Fine, then we got that far. Look, I haven't worked in two years, not really. There's nothing left for me to do. So—I'm putting myself on the line. (*She steps to the chorus line*) Yes, I'm putting myself on your line. I don't want to wait on tables. And what I really don't want to do is teach other people how to do what I should be doing myself. (*During song, lights dim out leaving her in spot*)
GOD, I'M A DANCER,
A DANCER DANCES!

CASSIE (Donna McKechnie): "THE MUSIC AND THE MIRROR"

Give me somebody to dance with.
Give me a place to fit in.
Help me return to the world of the living
By showing me how to begin.

Play me the music.
Give me the chance to come through.
All I ever needed was the music, and the mirror,
And the chance to dance for you.

Give me a job and you instantly get me involved.
If you give me a job,
Then the rest of the crap will get solved.
Put me to work,
You would think that by now I'm allowed.
I'll do you proud.

Throw me a rope to grab on to.
Help me to prove that I'm strong.
Give me the chance to look forward to sayin':
"Hey, listen, they're playing my song."

Play me the music.
Give me the chance to come through.
All I ever needed was the music, and the mirror,
And the chance to dance . . .
     (*Mirrors are now turned. Dance section*)
Play me the music,
Play me the music,
Play me the music.
Give me the chance to come through.
All I ever needed was the music, and the mirror,
And the chance to dance . . .

     (*Flying mirrors are used during this dance section. At the end of the number the stage is again black, music under*)

ZACH: You can't go back to the chorus, Cassie. That's not the answer.

CASSIE: I'm not trying to go back—I'm trying to start over again, Zach. I'll settle for that—starting over.

ZACH: Starting over . . . ? We can't . . .

CASSIE: What?—We? . . . You're talking about . . .

ZACH: No. I'm not.

CASSIE: Yes, you are. You're talking about us.

ZACH: Cassie, let's just keep this business, okay?

CASSIE: By all means. Well, who is here for anything else? That's what it's all about, isn't it? Work, Zach? Well, that's why I'm here today—about work.

ZACH: Well, you shouldn't have come. You don't fit in. You don't dance like anybody else—you don't know how.

CASSIE: But I did years ago and I can do it again. You're not even letting me try? Please, just give me a chance.

LARRY (*Enters up right*): Ah, excuse me . . . ah . . . do you want the kids back now?

ZACH: Uh, no . . . No, take the kids down to the basement and teach them the lyric to that number . . .

(LARRY *starts to leave*)

Oh, and send Paul in . . .

(LARRY *goes off. To* CASSIE)

Alright, go with Larry and learn the lyric.

CASSIE: Thank you . . .

> (*After* CASSIE *exits up right,* PAUL *enters, tentatively, upstage, then* . . .)

PAUL: Ah, you wanted to see me?

ZACH: Yes, Paul . . . I really like the way you dance.

> (PAUL *shrugs*)

No, I mean it, so I figured we'd try this again. For one thing, if you're going to change your name—why go from a Puerto Rican name to an Italian one?

PAUL: 'Cause I don't look it . . . People say, "You don't look Puerto Rican, you don't look Puerto Rican." But I am.

ZACH: So you figured you looked Italian?

PAUL: No, I, ah—just wanted to be somebody new. So I became Paul San Marco.

ZACH: Why did you want to become someone new?

PAUL: Why? I'm not exactly proud of my past.

> (*Music fades out*)

ZACH: Who is? But that's what the word means, Paul. Past.

PAUL: That might be easy for you to say, but . . .

ZACH: Look, wait a minute—what made you start dancing, your parents?

PAUL (*Begins to move to down stage center*): No, what do Puerto Ricans know about theatre? Now they have Channel Forty-Seven—but then they didn't have anything. But my father loved movies. And he'd take us all the time. He worked nights and he'd come home and take us to Forty-Second Street. And we'd come out of one movie and go to another and another movie—I don't know why—but I loved musicals.

ZACH: How old were you?

PAUL: Seven or eight.

ZACH: On Forty-Second Street?

PAUL: Yeah—it was a trip.

ZACH: Go on . . .

PAUL: I'd have to move down front—'cause I couldn't see—I wear contact lenses now . . . I'd move down front and these strange men would come and sit beside me and "play" with me. I never told anyone because—well, I guess it didn't matter . . .

ZACH: Why didn't it matter?

PAUL: Why? Ah . . . Well . . .

ZACH: Look, Paul, if this is too rough for you, I have your picture and resume . . .

PAUL (*He is down center on the line*): No. Ah . . . Okay. From seeing all those movie musicals, I used to dance around on the street, and I'd get caught all the time. God, it was embarrassing. I was always being Cyd Charisse . . . Always. Which I don't really understand, because I always wanted to be an actor. I mean, I really wanted to perform. Once my cousin said to me, "You'll never be an actor," and I knew she was telling me this because I was such a sissy. I mean, I was terribly effeminate. I always knew I was gay, but that didn't bother me. What bothered me was that I didn't know how to be a boy.

One day I looked at myself in the mirror and said, "You're fourteen years old and you're a faggot. What are you going to do with your life?" By that time I was in Cardinal Hayes High School. There were three thousand boys there. I had no protection any more. No homeroom where I could be charming and funny with the tough guys so they'd fight my battles for me. Like when I went to small schools. I liked school. But my grades got so bad. Even if I knew the answers to questions, I wouldn't raise my hand because I would be afraid they would laugh at me. They'd even whistle at me in the halls. It was awful . . . just awful. Finally, I went down to the Principal's office and said: "I'm a homosexual." Well, it was a Catholic high school at around nineteen sixty-two and at the age of fifteen you just didn't say that. He said: "Would you like to see a psychologist?" And I did. And he said: "I think you're very well-adjusted for your age and I think you should quit school." So, I did. But I didn't really want to. I couldn't take it anymore.

See, when I quit school, what I was doing was trying to find out who I was and how to be a man. You know, there are a lot of people in this world who don't know how to be men. And since then, I found out that I am one. I was looking for the wrong thing. I was trying to learn how to be butch. Anyway, I started hanging around Seventy-Second Street, meeting all these really strange people. Just trying to make friends that were like me. So that I'd understand what it was that I was.

PAUL (Sammy Williams): "You know, there are a lot of people in this world who don't know how to be a man."

Somebody told me they were looking for male dancers for the Jewel Box Revue, you know, the drag show. So, I go down to audition. Now, from all those years of pretending I was Cyd Charisse, I had this fabulous extension. I mean I could turn . . . anything my first audition. And they said to me: "You're too short to be a boy, would you like to be a pony?" And I said: "What's that?" And they said: "A girl." "What do I have to do?" "Show us your legs." "But I have hair on my legs." "That's okay, come on upstairs." So I went and they hiked up my dungarees and they put on a pair of nylon stockings and high heels. It was freaky. It was incredible. And then they brought me back downstairs and they said: "Oh, you have wonderful legs." I said: "Really? . . . Terrific . . . "

It's so strange thinking about this. It was a whole lifetime ago. I was just past sixteen. Anyway, then there was this thing of me trying to hide it from my parents. That was something. 'Cause I had to buy all this stuff. Like, ah, shoes to rehearse in, earrings, makeup. And I would hide it all and my mother would find it. I told her there was this girl in the show and she didn't want her mother to know what she was doing and I was holding this stuff for her. She believed me.

Well, I was finally in show business. It was the asshole of show business—but it was a job . . . Nothing to brag about. I had friends. But after a while it was so demeaning. Nobody at the Jewel Box had any dignity and most of them were ashamed of themselves and considered themselves freaks. I don't know, I think it was the lack of dignity that got to me, so I left. Oh, I muddled around for a while. I worked as an office boy, a waiter—But without an education, you can't get a good job. So, when the Jewel Box called and asked if I'd come back, I went.

We were working the Apollo Theatre on a Hundred and Twenty-

Fifth Street. Doing four shows a day with a movie. It was really tacky. The show was going to go to Chicago. My parents wanted to say goodbye and they were going to bring my luggage to the theatre after the show. Well, we were doing this oriental number and I looked like Anna May Wong. I had these two great big chrysanthemums on either side of my head and a huge headdress with gold balls hanging all over it. I was going on for the finale and going down the stairs and who should I see standing by the stage door . . . my parents. They got there too early. I freaked. I didn't know what to do. I thought to myself: "I know, I'll just walk quickly past them like all the others and they'll never recognize me." So I took a deep breath and started down the stairs and just as I passed my mother I heard her say: "Oh, my God." Well . . . I died. But what could I do? I had to go on for the finale so I just kept going. After the show I went back to my dressing room and after I'd finished dressing and taking my makeup off, I went back down stairs. And there they were standing in the middle of all these . . . And all they said to me was please write, make sure you eat and take care of yourself. And just before my parents left, my father turned to the producer and said: "Take care of my son . . . " That was the first time he ever called me that . . . I . . . ah . . . I . . . ah. (*He breaks down*)

> (*Music under, during which* ZACH *comes down the aisle and up on stage, crosses to* PAUL, *puts an arm around his shoulder and walks a few steps up left talking to him but we don't hear*)

LARRY (*Entering from right*): Zach, you ready for them yet?

> (ZACH *signals "no" with his hand, continues to talk to* PAUL, *then . . .* ZACH *drops hand. Music under*)

ZACH: Alright, bring 'em in.

> (*Crosses to stool down right.* PAUL *crosses to first wing right and drops his dance bag*)

Photo by Martha Swope

PAUL (Sammy Williams), ZACH (Robert LuPone), CASSIE (Donna McKechnie), VAL (Pamela Blair), DIANA (Priscilla Lopez) and SHEILA (Carole Bishop) rehearse "ONE"

LARRY: Okay, kids, here we go.

> (*The rest of the group enters up right. Upstage black panels revolve to mirrors as they enter*)

ZACH: Larry, get the hats.

> (LARRY *and* PAUL *pull a box of hats on stage,* ZACH *gets his own hat from under stool*)

LARRY: We're using hats. Everybody grab a hat. Try to find one that fits.

ZACH (*To* LARRY): Alright, let's review this.

> (*The group all grabs hats and begins warming up, going over lyrics, commenting on hats, etc., while* LARRY *and* ZACH *are reviewing the combination facing the mirrors. When* PAUL *and* RICHIE *take the hat box off,* ZACH *crosses down center and group forms around him*)

Alright. This is the same combination we worked on earlier, it also goes with the lyrics you just learned. Now—this is important! I want to see *Unison Dancing*. Every head, arm, body angle, *exactly the same*. You must blend. This is one of those numbers where you back the star—you're her frame. I don't want anybody to pull my eye. Now, let's review it.

> (ZACH, LARRY *and group face mirrors*)

Starting position is turned-in third. Hips and shoulders on the diagonal. Elbows up, chest up, chin up, eyes front. Ready? A-five, six, seven, eight, a-"One." Change. Walk, walk. Point. Point. Point. Flick. Step. Kick. (*He stops dancing*) Okay, let's do it again. From "Singular sensation." And . . .

MIKE, AL, DON and MAGGIE (*Sing*):
SINGULAR SENSATION

(ZACH *continues with demonstration dialogue {see his following speech} as singing continues*)

Ev'ry little step she takes.
One thrilling combination
Ev'ry move that she makes.
One smile and suddenly nobody else will do.
You know you'll never be lonely with you know who.

One moment in her presence
And you can forget the rest.
For the girl is second best to none, son.
Ooh! Sigh!
Give her your attention.
Do I
Really have to mention
She's the one?

zach: Point and point and point. Flick, step, kick, step change. Continuing . . . Walk, walk, up, down, up, down, down, point, down, point, step, brush, step, brush, step, brush, back, back, back, flick, step and step and step, lunge, lunge. Slow, three four five six, hat, kick, step, brush, with the arm, step, brush back, back, arm down, lift, lift, lift, change. Step and step, on the angle, step and step, body square. (*Beat*) Back, down, step, point, make it sharp, body square, on the angle. Back, cross, back, back, cross, step, step, ball change. Hat to the head, step touch, step up, step up, plié, kick, plié, tip the hat, plié, tip the hat, plié . . . right, ball change, kick. (*Beat*) Hat, no hat, hat, no hat, hat, hat, hat, hat. (*Walking down center*) Now, let's do the whole combination, facing away from the mirror.

mike: Excuse me, but after we do the grapevine step, the hat comes down on two?

ZACH: Yeah. Hats on two.

JUDY: But when do you bring the hat up?

LARRY (*Demonstrating*): It's on five. One, two, three, four, FIVE, six, seven, eight, one, TWO . . .

ZACH: Listen, now listen.

> (*They group around* ZACH)

. . . now Larry has the exact style I'm looking for, very thirties. Everyone keep your eye on him. Let's do it again. A-*five, six, seven, eight*, a . . .

> (ZACH *goes into pantomime; lights change*)

GREG: One

MARK: Two . . .

KRISTINE: Shoulder up . . .

MIKE:
     SINGULAR SENSATION . . .

KRISTINE: Stay pulled up . . .

BEBE: Point . . .

PAUL: And . . .

BEBE: Point . . .

PAUL: Flick . . .

BEBE: Step, kick . . .

VAL: Hat to the head . . .

BOBBY: Three, four . . .

JUDY: Lead with the hip—follow through . . .

SHEILA: Up, down . . .

DIANA: Fill the phrase . . .

VAL: Elbow right . . .

MAGGIE: Down, point . . .

DON: Step, brush . . .

MARK: Three, four . . .

RICHIE:
     SUDDENLY NOBODY

BEBE: Step, flick . . .

SHEILA: Step, up, step, and step . . .

PAUL: Lunge . . .

CONNIE: Lunge . . .

JUDY: Slow . . .

MARK: Three, four, five, six . . .

KRISTINE: Hat . . .

MIKE: Kick . . .

DON: Step, brush . . .

JUDY: Palm up . . .

MARK: Five, six . . .

GREG: Back, back . . .

> (*Suddenly the individual voices blend into a collage of four groups. As one group counts, another sings the refrain, while two other groups are speaking the following simultaneously*)

JUDY, DIANA, KRISTINE and VAL (*Spoken*):

Lift, elbow straight, pose,
angle to the left and
change to the right, palm
up, hat-head and
hat-right, hat-chest
hat-right, hat-chest,
body right, eyes front,
body straight, hat-up,
down to the head, other side,
stay pulled up, shoulder up,
tip the hat, tip the hat,
tip the hat, tip the hat,
hat-up, hat-hold,
(*beat*) up, (*beat*) hold,
(*beat*) up, (*beat*) up,
(*beat*) up, (*beat*) up.

MAGGIE, SHEILA, BEBE and CONNIE (*Spoken*):

Lift, lift, lift, change,
step and step . . .
Step and step, up,
cross, back, front, step,
down, point, down, point,
down, point, down, point,
back, cross, back, back,
cross, back step, ball change,
step, touch, step, touch,
step, up, step, up,
plié, kick, plié, kick,
plié, kick, plié, kick,
ball change, kick, step, kick,
step, kick, step, kick,
step, kick, step, kick,
step, kick, step, kick.

MIKE, GREG, DON and AL (*Sing*):	BOBBY, MARK, RICHIE and PAUL (*Spoken*):
ONE	One, two, three, four,
MOMENT IN HER PRESENCE	five, six, seven, eight.
AND YOU CAN FORGET THE	One, two, three, four,
REST.	five, six, seven, eight.
FOR THE GIRL IS SECOND	One, two, three, four,
BEST TO	five, six, seven, eight.
NONE,	One, two, three, four,
SON.	five, six, seven, eight.
OOH! SIGH!	One, two, three, four,
GIVE HER YOUR ATTENTION.	five, six, seven, eight.
DO I	One, two, three, four,
REALLY HAVE TO MENTION	five, six, seven, eight.
SHE'S	One, two, three, four,
THE	five, six, seven, eight.
ONE?	One, two, three, four,
	five, six, seven, eight.

(They finish the combination. The lights come back up)

ZACH: Right. Let's do it in groups of four. First group ready? Group one.

(Again the lights change)

A-five, six, seven, eight. Group two. Group three. Group four.

(Again the lights change. As ZACH starts each group, they speak the following. The underlined phrases are spoken more loudly than the others as in a 'round')

MIKE, GREG, DON and AL (*Sing*):

ONE

SINGULAR SENSATION   BOBBY, MARK, RICHIE and PAUL

EV'RY LITTLE STEP SHE   (*Spoken*):

<u>One</u>, <u>two</u>, <u>three</u>, <u>four</u>,

TAKES.
ONE
THRILLING COMBINATION
EV'RY MOVE THAT SHE
MAKES.

ONE SMILE AND
SUDDENLY NOBODY
ELSE WILL
DO.
YOU KNOW YOU'LL
NEVER BE LONELY WITH
YOU KNOW
WHO.

ONE
MOMENT IN HER PRESENCE
AND YOU CAN FORGET THE
REST.
FOR THE GIRL IS SECOND
BEST TO
NONE,
SON.

OOH! SIGH!
GIVE HER YOUR ATTENTION.
DO I
REALLY HAVE TO MENTION
SHE'S
THE
ONE?

five, six, seven, eight.
One, two three, four,
five, six, seven, eight.
One, two, three, four,
five, six, seven, eight.

One, two, three, four,
five, six, seven, eight.
One, two, three, four,
five, six, seven, eight.
One, two, three, four,
five, six, seven, eight.
One, two, three, four,
five, six, seven, eight.

One, two, three, four,
five, six, seven, eight.
One, two, three, four,
five, six, seven, eight.
One, two, three, four,
five, six, seven, eight.
One, two, three, four.
five, six, seven, eight.

One, two, three, four,
five, six, seven, eight.
One, two, three, four,
five, six, seven, eight.
One, two, three, four,
five, six, seven, eight.
One, two, three, four,
five, six, seven, eight.

MAGGIE, SHEILA, BEBE and
CASSIE (*Spoken*):
> One, change,
> step, (*beat*) step, (*beat*)
> point, (*beat*) point, (*beat*)
> point, flick, step, kick,
> touch, change,
> walk, (*beat*) walk, (*beat*)
> up, down, up, down,
> down, point, down, point,
> step, brush, step, brush,
> step brush, back, back,
> step, flick, step, up,
> step and step, lunge . . .
> lunge, slow . . .
> hat, kick,
> step, brush, step, brush,

JUDY, DIANA, KRISTINE and VAL
(*Spoken*):
> One, hat, shoulder up,
> walk, (*beat*) walk, (*beat*)
> stay pulled up, eyes front,
> hat to chest, angle right
> hat to the head,
> lead with the hip, follow thru;
> palm up, fill the phrase,
> elbow right, hat down,
> hat to chest, elbow up,
> change the body,
> leave the head, shoulder left,
> head, lead to the right, hat
> up, knee in, elbow

> down, hat to the head, kick,
> lift the arm, palm up,
> fill the phrase, arm down,
> lift, elbow straight, pose,
> angle to the left and
> change to the right, pull
> up, hat-head, and
> hat-right, hat-chest,

> step, brush, back, back,
> lift, lift, lift, change,
> step and step, (*beat*)
> step and step, up
> cross, back, front, step,
> down, point, down, point,
> down, point, down, point,
> back, cross, back, back,

> hat-right, hat-chest,
> body right, eyes front,
> body straight, hat-up,
> down to the head, other side,
> stay pulled up, shoulder up,
> tip the hat, tip the hat,
> tip the hat, tip the hat,

> cross, back, step, ball change,
> step, touch, step, touch,
> step, up, step, up,
> plié, kick, plié, kick,
> plié, kick, plié, kick,
> ball change, kick, step, kick,
> step, kick, step, kick,

<u>hat-up, hat-hold.</u>   <u>step, kick, step, kick.</u>

(*Lights back to reality*)

ZACH: Right—Let me see the girls in a line. The tallest girls in the center, shorter girls on the ends. A-five, six . . .

(*Music under. Girls are in line with boys holding upstage of them*)

CASSIE: I don't have a hat.

ZACH: Hold it. Larry, a hat.

BOBBY (*Handing a hat to* CASSIE): Here, Cassie.

CASSIE: Oh, thanks.

ZACH: A-five, six, seven, eight, a-one, change.

GIRLS (*Plus offstage girls; sing*):
   ONE . . .

ZACH (*To* CASSIE): You're late.

GIRLS (*Sing*):
   SINGULAR SENSATION
   EV'RY LITTLE STEP SHE TAKES,

ZACH (*To* SHEILA): Straighten the supporting leg, Sheila.

GIRLS (*Sing*):
   ONE . . .

ZACH: Don't pop the head, Cassie.

GIRLS (*Sing*):
>   THRILLING COMBINATION,

ZACH: Maggie, make it sharper.

GIRLS (*Sing*):
>   EV'RY MOVE THAT SHE MAKES,

ZACH: Too high with the leg, Cassie.

GIRLS (*Sing*):
>   ONE SMILE AND SUDDENLY NOBODY ELSE WILL DO . . .

ZACH: Too much plié, Cassie.

GIRLS (*Sing*):
>   YOU KNOW YOU'LL NEVER BE LONELY WITH YOU KNOW WHO . . .

ZACH: Eyes front, Val.

GIRLS (*Sing*):
>   ONE MOMENT IN HER PRESENCE,
>   AND YOU CAN FORGET THE REST . . .

ZACH: You're late on the turn, Cassie.

GIRLS (*Sing*):
>   FOR THE GIRL IS SECOND BEST
>   TO NONE, SON . . .
>   OOH! SIGH! GIVE HER YOUR ATTENTION

ZACH: Don't pop the hip, Cassie.

GIRLS (*Sing*):
> DO I REALLY HAVE TO MENTION
> SHE'S . . . THE . . . ONE?

ZACH: That's good placement, Sheila. Alright, boys.

> (*Boys are in line with girls holding upstage*)

BOYS (*Plus offstage boys; sing*):
> ONE . . .

ZACH: Do it again, Cassie.

BOYS (*Sing*):
> SINGULAR SENSATION
> EV'RY LITTLE STEP SHE TAKES . . .

ZACH: Six, seven eight, one . . .

BOYS (*Sing*):
> ONE . . .

ZACH: Don't pop the head, Cassie.

BOYS (*Sing*):
> THRILLING COMBINATION
> EV'RY MOVE THAT SHE MAKES.
> ONE SMILE AND SUDDENLY NOBODY ELSE WILL DO
> YOU KNOW YOU'LL NEVER BE LONELY WITH YOU KNOW WHO.
>
> ONE . . . MOMENT IN HER PRESENCE
> AND YOU CAN FORGET THE REST.

ZACH (*Shouting*): You're distorting the combination, Cassie. Pull in. Cool it. Dance like everybody else.

BOYS (*Sing*):
>   FOR THE GIRL IS SECOND BEST
>   TO NONE . . . SON.
>   OOH! SIGH! GIVE HER YOUR ATTENTION.
>   DO I REALLY HAVE TO MENTION
>   SHE'S THE ONE?

>   (*The boys and girls form a single line*)

ZACH: Alright, now everyone in line and SMILE AND SING!

ALL (*Including offstage singers*):
>   ONE SINGULAR SENSATION
>   EV'RY LITTLE STEP SHE TAKES.
>   ONE . . . THRILLING COMBINATION
>   EV'RY MOVE THAT SHE MAKES.
>   ONE SMILE AND SUDDENLY NOBODY ELSE WILL DO,
>   YOU KNOW YOU'LL NEVER BE LONELY WITH YOU KNOW WHO.

>   ONE MOMENT IN HER PRESENCE
>   AND YOU CAN FORGET THE REST.
>   FOR THE GIRL IS SECOND BEST
>   TO NONE, SON.
>   OOH! SIGH! GIVE HER YOUR ATTENTION.
>   DO I REALLY HAVE TO MENTION
>   SHE'S THE . . .
>>   (ZACH *pulls* CASSIE *from the line, brings her downstage left*)
>   ONE?

>>   (*The group begins to chant softly the first half of the refrain with* ZACH/CASSIE *dialogue over. They have backed up*)

CASSIE: What's wrong? What are you doing?

ZACH: My job.

THE COMPANY:
ONE SINGULAR SENSATION—etc.

CASSIE: What?

ZACH: How can you do it? You got out of the chorus when you were twenty-two—what the hell makes you think you can go back when you're thirty-two?

CASSIE: My sanity.

ZACH: Cassie, you can't do it.

CASSIE: But I did it. I did what you wanted. I pulled in—I cooled it— I danced like everybody else.

ZACH: I know you did. And to be perfectly honest—I couldn't stand it.

THE COMPANY:
YOU KNOW YOU'LL NEVER—etc.

CASSIE: You know, that's *your* problem. Why? Because you took me out of the chorus in the first place? Does that make you feel like some kind of failure?

(*She starts to run off stage right; she stops when he speaks*)

ZACH: Why did you leave me?

CASSIE: Oh, so we are gonna get into that?

ZACH: Why did you leave me? I came home one night and you were gone.

CASSIE (Donna McKechnie) to ZACH (Robert LuPone): "And you were in love with it and off in the only world that means anything to you."

CASSIE: Why, Zach—you noticed.

ZACH: Very funny.

CASSIE: You'd already left me weeks before.

ZACH: Left? I thought we were living together?

CASSIE: No, sharing the same apartment, maybe. No, I mean, in the real sense of the word—left. You left. Well, you were madly in love again and . . .

ZACH (*Crossing in*): I wasn't, you know I wasn't. I was directing my first play.

CASSIE: And you were in love with it and off in the only world that means anything to you.

ZACH: Cassie, you know how important it was to me. Christ, if I could direct a straight play and pull it off, it meant I wasn't going to be stuck just making up dance steps the rest of my life.

(*He is at center, she is still stage right*)

CASSIE: Oh, you were never gonna be stuck. You were gonna make sure you did it all—direct, choreograph—musicals, plays, movies . . . I knew you loved work—but you really get off on it, don't you?

ZACH: Yeah . . . I guess I do. You didn't seem to mind it when we were working together. It was only when we weren't that—

(*He has now crossed to her*)

CASSIE: Oh, Zach, I didn't mind not being part of your work. I loved you, I could have handled that. It was not being a part of your life that got to me. And not being able to keep up with you. Because that's what you expected. I know you did. You were moving up and you wanted me to be right there with you. Well, I was a good dancer, but you wanted me to be a star.

ZACH: What's wrong with that? Why shouldn't you be? Why shouldn't you be the best you can be? I decided I was going to . . .

CASSIE: That's not a decision, that's a disease. God, good, better, best!—I hate it! How can you stand it? Are you gonna go from one show to the next to the next rehearsing them all twenty-four hours a day for the rest of your life? You know, you're not even doing it for yourself. You're trying to prove something. Like I was—because I was doing it for you, to please you, to keep you—to get you back. But I don't want to prove anything anymore. I want to do what I love as much as I can and as long as I can. But at least, now—I'm doing it for me. Who are you doing it for?

CHORUS (Sings):
ONE SINGULAR SENSATION

CHORUS (Mouths):
EV'RY LITTLE STEP SHE TAKES

CASSIE: I'm sorry. I have no right to judge.

CHORUS (Sings):
ONE THRILLING COMBINATION

CHORUS (Mouths):
EV'RY MOVE THAT SHE MAKES

CASSIE: Why are we doing this? I mean, we must be over this by now, aren't we?

(He crosses to stage left, turns back to her)

CHORUS *(Sings)*:
    ONE SMILE AND SUDDENLY
    NOBODY ELSE WILL DO

ZACH: I am.

CHORUS *(Mouths)*:
    YOU KNOW YOU'LL NEVER BE LONELY
    WITH YOU KNOW WHO

CASSIE: Good. Then don't feel you owe me any favors. *(She crosses to center)* . . . Just treat me like everybody else.

ZACH: Is that what you really want from me? *(Pointing to the line)* Is this really what you want to do?

    (They both look upstage at the line as it slowly comes to life. The music builds)

CHORUS *(With offstage singers)*:
    ONE MOMENT IN HER PRESENCE
    AND YOU CAN FORGET THE REST.
    FOR THE GIRL IS SECOND BEST
    TO NONE, SON.
    OOH! SIGH! GIVE HER YOUR ATTENTION.
    DO I REALLY HAVE TO MENTION
    SHE'S . . .
    THE . . .
    ONE?
        (Loud)
    ONE . . . ONE . . . ONE . . . ONE . . .
        (Soft)
    ONE . . . ONE . . . ONE . . . ONE . . .

(Line begins backing up and begins counting eight counts of eight softly under dialogue below. The mirrors turn to black and the line faces upstage and passes hats off up right. The last count of eight is done silently as they get into place for the tap combination)

CASSIE: Yes . . . I'd be proud to be one of them. They're wonderful.

ZACH: But you're special.

CASSIE: No, we're all special. He's special—she's special. And Sheila—and Richie, and Connie. They're all special. I'd be happy to be dancing in that line. Yes, I would . . . and I'll take chorus . . . if you'll take me. *(She runs up right)*

LARRY *(Who has been down right, crosses to ZACH center)*: Alright, who are we going to hire?

ZACH: I don't know.

LARRY: Well, what do you want to do now?

ZACH *(Crossing to his stool and throws hat off down right)*: Start matching them up. Do the tap combination.

LARRY *(To the group)*: Okay, the tap combination. A-five, six, seven, eight . . .

(ZACH sits on stool. The group reviews the tap combination. During the routine, several people sing inner thoughts which follow. Each is picked up in a head spot)

SHEILA:
GOD, WHEN IT'S OVER DO I NEED A DRINK!

MIKE:
HE'S GOTTA KNOW WHAT HE WANTS BY NOW.

BEBE:

Oh, Jesus, have I got a headache!

MAGGIE:

I'm not sure I can smile much longer.

JUDY:

I shoulda been a singer . . .
   (*Bad soprano-like high note*)
"AAAAHH!"
   (*Exasperated*)
Well . . .

BOBBY:

If George Hamilton can be a movie star,
Then I could be a movie star.

AL:

What am I doing in show business?

LARRY: Okay, everybody stage right, please.

   (*They go to stage right and continue to follow* LARRY's *instruction*)

I'm going to put you into couples now. Let me see, I'll start with
. . . Ah . . . Don, Judy, Bobby and Kristine. Oh, no, girls work on
the other side of the boys. Sheila and Bebe, stand by. Boys work
upstage a bit. A-five, six, seven, eight . . .

   (*Music cue for dance section. The first group begins the
   combination*)

Don, try working a little closer to Judy . . . Stay on the beat . . .

   (*They continue dancing until* LARRY *stops them*)

Okay, hold it . . . Judy and Kristine stage left, boys stay . . . Let me see Sheila with Don and Bebe dance with Bobby . . . A-five, six, seven, eight . . .

(*Music cue for dance section. They begin the combination*)

Let me see some smiles . . . Not that phony "Sell-smile," I want to see that "I-love-to-dance smile."

(SHEILA *overdoes it—they complete the combination*)

Okay, alright, stage left, now, let me see . . . Diana here with Greg . . . Valerie . . . Mark, dance with Val.

VAL: Smile, honey.

LARRY: A-five, six, seven, eight . . .

(*Music cue for dance section. They dance*)

Diana, I'm not hearing any taps.

DIANA: It's my sneakers . . . (*She pounds the floor, trying to make tap sounds with her sneakers*)

LARRY: Stay on the beat . . .

(*They complete the combination*)

Okay, kids, stage left . . . Ah, Maggie and . . . (*To* MIKE) Mark . . .

MIKE: Mike . . .

LARRY: And Connie, are you hiding back there? Come out here.

CONNIE (*Running into position*) Tapping is not my strongest point . . .

LARRY: And give me . . . Paul. Other three hang on . . . A-five, six, seven, eight . . .

(*Music cue for dance section. They begin the combination*)

Boys, hold upstage of the girls . . . Connie, relax, loosen up, enjoy it.

(CONNIE *dances like a noodle. They continue to dance until* PAUL *falls while doing a turn. Music fades out fast when* PAUL *falls*)

MAGGIE: Connie!

(*Stops* CONNIE *dancing*)

MIKE (*Going to* PAUL): Paul! Get up, Paul . . .

BOBBY (*Crosses to* PAUL, *supports his shoulders. To* MIKE): Hey, what are you doing?

MIKE: What do you mean, I'm just trying . . .

(*Others are crowding around*)

PAUL: Oh, Jesus!

BOBBY: Are you okay?

PAUL: Yeah, yeah . . . (*He moans*)

ZACH: Paul, you okay? Did you hurt yourself? (*Crosses to him and kneels*)

PAUL: No, no, I—it's just, ah . . .

ZACH: Did you pull a muscle? Is it your ankle?

DIANA: It's not your knee, is it?

PAUL: Ah . . .

Photo by Martha Swope

PAUL's accident

ZACH (*To* DIANA): An old injury?

DIANA: Yeah, he just had it operated on last year. It's his cartilage.

SHEILA: Oh, shit . . .

ZACH: Stand back . . . Give him some air . . .

>   (*They move back*)

CASSIE (*Crossing to them*): Call a doctor.

PAUL: No, really . . .

CASSIE (*To* ZACH): You should call a doctor.

ZACH: Paul, who's your doctor?

PAUL: I don't want a doctor.

ZACH: Paul, who's your doctor?

CASSIE: Call Sidney Rhodes. 595-7639.

ZACH: Larry, call him.

>   (LARRY *starts upstage right*)

CASSIE (*Following* LARRY *to exit*): Doctor Sidney Rhodes, 595-7639.

ZACH (*Sotto voce*): Paul, just try to breathe in slowly and relax.

CASSIE: You know, maybe you should prop something under his knee . . .

ZACH: Give me a dance bag.

(MAGGIE *crosses right and gets a bag*)

PAUL: No, it's okay. I think I just twisted it.

(MAGGIE *returns and hands the bag to* ZACH)

ZACH: Easy, ready . . . up. (*He slides the bag under* PAUL's *knee*)

PAUL: Oh, shit . . .

ZACH: Is that better?

CASSIE: Does anybody have a Darvon or a Valium?

SHEILA: I do. (*She crosses left to her dance bag*)

ZACH: Somebody get me some water.

MARK: I will! (*He runs off right*)

ZACH: You're gonna be okay, Paul.

PAUL: Yeah, but out of work, huh?

> (SHEILA *crosses to* ZACH *with pills and* MARK *comes back with a cup of water*)

MAGGIE: Look, I don't think you should give him that. You don't know what's wrong.

SHEILA: Please, I've had three already today.

LARRY (*returning from off right*): Zach, the doctor said it'd be quicker if we got him into a cab and over to St. Joseph's Hospital than if he came here—He'll be waiting for him at the emergency entrance.

ZACH: Right. (*Looking around*) Ah . . .

CASSIE: I'll go.

ZACH: No.

DON: I'll help you.

ZACH: Fine.

>   (DON *and* BOBBY *cross to help* PAUL *up*)

Let's get him up. Ready, one, two, three.

>   (*They lift him up and start up right*)

LARRY (*Following them*): Where's his dance bag?

GREG: Which is his?

>   (VAL *hands him bag which he puts on* LARRY's *shoulder*)

ZACH (*Following them to exit*): Paul, I'll see you later. (*To* LARRY) Call me from the hospital.

>   (*They exit up right. The group stands silently,* ZACH *crosses back downstage, looks at* CASSIE, *who turns and crosses down left. At top of steps he turns and then . . .*)

ZACH: What do you do when you can't dance anymore?

BEBE: Kill yourself.

ZACH: No, really.

DIANA: Oh, shit, what kind of a question is that?

GREG: Real heavy.

MARK: Yeah.

ZACH: I know, but what do you do?

RICHIE (*After a long beat, crosses from up left to center*): I'll tell ya. Because I'm getting scared. I love being in this business. But, one day it hits you, "Okay, Richie, you been havin' fun for almost eight years now . . . but where's it gettin' you?"

AL (*Crossing to him*): A lot of people are feeling that way. And they're getting out of the business fast.

RICHIE: Well, there's no security in dancing.

JUDY: But wait a second . . .

RICHIE: There's no promotion and no advancement.

DIANA: Listen, if you're looking for that kind of security . . . forget it.

RICHIE: No, it's not just that.

DIANA: Well, what then?

RICHIE: I could do without that, but—shit—there's no work anymore.

(*Whole group reacts simultaneously with similar lines. All lines are spoken at the same time—together with the next three lines*)

MIKE: Tell me about it.

CONNIE: It's true.

GREG: Sure it is . . . but isn't that happening to every . . .

(ZACH *goes down to bottom of steps and faces stage*)

BEBE (*Stopping group and crossing down to line*): Oh, please—I don't wanna hear about how Broadway's dying. 'Cause I just got here.

BOBBY: Don't worry, honey—it's not.

CONNIE: They're not doing big musicals like they used to.

MIKE: But even if they did—even if you get *this* show . . . it's gonna close one day—nothin' runs forever, right?

DIANA: Yeah, sure—but that's . . . just the way it is . . .

AL (*Overlapping end of* DIANA's *line above*): He's right.

RICHIE: And then you have to start all over again—'cause the only chorus line you can depend on in this business is the one at un-em-ploy-ment!

> (*Group reacts simultaneously—all lines spoken on top of each other—together with next three lines*)

CONNIE: Hit it, Richie.

BOBBY: Oh, please, give me a break.

DON: Well, look, it's . . .

JUDY (*Crossing in to group center*): But don't you want to do more than just dance in the chorus?

MARK: Gee, I just want to get in one.

JUDY: Well, I want to be something besides the tall, skinny, redhead second from the end. Not that I want to be a star or anything.

VAL: Hell, I do.

SHEILA: Oh, who doesn't. Everybody in the whole goddam country wants to be a star.

JUDY (*Crosses downstage to talk to* ZACH): Okay—I admit it. I wanna be the next Gwen Verdon.

ZACH: But she dances.

JUDY: I know—Don't you just love her?

ZACH: But I want to know what you're going to do when you can't dance anymore.

(JUDY *crosses upstage and sits on floor*)

VAL (*Crossing down to talk to* ZACH): Who cares? I don't care if I never dance another step as long as I live. I'd be happy just going to Hollywood and replacing Jill St. John. Big fucking deal, right? Well, I can dream, can't I?

DON (*Crossing down to her*): Yeah, but dreams don't pay the rent.

VAL: So . . . I'll find somebody who can.

MIKE (*Crossing to them*): That's the thing that gets me—a girl can always get married.

SHEILA: She didn't say anything about marriage.

MIKE (*To* SHEILA): Another thing is . . .

BEBE (*Seated on floor on line left center*): Oh, please, I don't know if I can take it.

MIKE: These bodies don't last forever . . .

BEBE: I can't take it.

MIKE (*To* ZACH): We're no better off than athletes.

BOBBY (*Crossing down to* VAL's *right*): Well, I'm sorry—I can't worry about any of that now. 'Cause I plan to go on kicking these legs as long as I can and when I can't . . . Well, I'll just do something else.

VAL: Right. So you get into acting.

(*Group reacts—positively and negatively*)

No, you'll love it. I mean, it's fabulous to find out you can talk too. That's what I'm into . . . not very good . . . but I'm getting better. And I'll tell ya somethin', honey, it beats busting your ass dancing any day. And at least, when you're an actor you stand a chance.

AL: Aw, come on, there are more actors outta work than dancers.

DIANA: Oh shit—that's theatre! Listen, nobody got into this business to play it safe. And we're all here because we wanted to be here and you're all acting like it's just another job—and it's not. So, what are you all talking about? (*Crosses upstage center*)

GREG: LIFE! Darlings. It's tough all over. That's why I have no plans, no alternatives—just get me through the day . . . one day at a time is enough for me to deal with.

(GREG *crosses back to right portal,* RICHIE *sits upstage left.* DON *crosses down to talk to* ZACH)

DON: Listen, we all feel the same way or we wouldn't be here. But I have a wife and two kids, and as much as I love dancin' and the-atre—it's all about paying the bills now, and getting the kids through school. I mean, I have to go where the money is.

ZACH: What are you going to do?

DON: Well, I'd like to stay in the business . . . maybe stage managing . . . someday directing . . .

VAL: Hello . . .

DON: Whatever, I'll just have to see.

(VAL *crosses upstage and sits*)

MAGGIE: Oh, I can't think of anything else I'd do.

BOBBY: Well, if we all had to pick another career . . . Go on, pick a career. (*Crossing to* SHEILA *stage left on line*) What would you like to be when you grow up.

SHEILA: Young!

CONNIE (*Crosses to center*): I know what I'm gonna do. Because I know—one night whatever show I'm in is gonna close and I'm finally gonna be able to go off my diet. Then I'm gonna get in the car with my husband, go up to our fifty acres in Vermont, have a bunch of kids, dance around my kitchen cooking and enjoy getting fat.

KRISTINE (*Up right with* AL): That sounds good—except the fat part. Yeah, I'd like that. Just not right away.

BOBBY: Listen, all I want to be is just happy.

DIANA: Aw, come on, aren't you happy? Look, I sit around and get depressed and worry about all these things, too. But then I meet somebody and they say to me: "Wow, you dance on Broadway! How fabulous! You got somewhere. You're something." And

Christ, I get this feeling—(*Music under*) inside because I remember when I used to stand outside of that stage door and watch all these girls come out of there, with their eyelashes and their make-up and I'd think: "God, I'll never be that old. I'll never be that old. I'll never be old enough to come out of that stage door." But deep down inside I knew I would and, goddam it, I've come this far and I'm not giving up now.

SHEILA (*Crossing up left center*): That's what I used to say . . . I won't give up. I've got to be a ballerina by the time I'm eighteen . . . Then I found out that I should be in musical comedy and I said: "Okay, I'll be a chorus girl—but I gotta be playing parts by the time I'm twenty-one."

DIANA: Oh no, did you do that too? Give yourself a time limit?

MAGGIE: I still do it.

SHEILA: Right. Then you're twenty-five and you say just a couple of years more—well, hell, I'm thirty. I mean how many years do I have left to be a chorus-cutie? Three? Four? If I have my eyes done . . . Well, I don't want to deal on that level any longer. So, just lately, I've been thinking about opening a dance studio. I don't know . . . Am I copping out? Am I growing up? I don't know . . .

DIANA: Who does? Listen, who knows anything? It's just something you're gonna have to wait and see.

ZACH (*He has made his way to the rear of the house*): Right.

(*Lights change for song, group looks front on light cue*)

But if today were the day you had to stop dancing. How would you feel?

"WHAT I D

OR LOVE"

DIANA (*Sings*):
>   KISS TODAY GOODBYE,
>   THE SWEETNESS AND THE SORROW.
>   WISH ME LUCK, THE SAME TO YOU,
>   BUT I CAN'T REGRET
>   WHAT I DID FOR LOVE, WHAT I DID FOR LOVE.
>
>   LOOK, MY EYES ARE DRY.
>   THE GIFT WAS OURS TO BORROW.
>   IT'S AS IF WE ALWAYS KNEW,
>   AND I WON'T FORGET WHAT I DID FOR LOVE,
>   WHAT I DID FOR LOVE.
>
>   GONE,
>   LOVE IS NEVER GONE.
>   AS WE TRAVEL ON,
>   LOVE'S WHAT WE'LL REMEMBER.
>
>   KISS TODAY GOODBYE,
>   AND POINT ME T'WARD TOMORROW.
>   WE DID WHAT WE HAD TO DO.
>   WON'T FORGET, CAN'T REGRET   GROUP:
>   WHAT I DID FOR LOVE.   LOVE.

ALL:
>   WHAT I DID FOR LOVE.   LOVE.

DIANA:
>   WHAT I DID FOR . . .

ALL (*Adding more voices each phrase*):
>   LOVE
>   LOVE IS NEVER GONE
>   AS WE TRAVEL ON

LOVE'S WHAT WE'LL REMEMBER
(*Offstage voices are added*):
KISS TODAY GOODBYE.

DIANA:
AND POINT ME T'WARD TOMORROW.

ALL:
POINT ME T'WARD TOMORROW.
WE DID WHAT WE HAD TO DO.
WON'T FORGET, CAN'T REGRET
WHAT I DID FOR LOVE.
WHAT I DID FOR LOVE.

DIANA:
WHAT I DID FOR . . .

ALL:
LOVE.

> (*Slowly in time to the vamp, they move facing back to line, first one, then two, then more, etc. When they are all back in line, leaving* PAUL's *position empty,* ZACH *speaks; piano solo under*)

ZACH: Before I start eliminating, I just want to say I think you're terrific. You've been wonderful about going through all of this today. I sincerely wish I could hire all of you, but I can't . . . Will the following people please step forward: Don . . . Greg . . . Al . . . Diana, no. (*To* DIANA) I'm wrong, back in line. (*To others*) . . . Kristine . . . Bebe . . . Sheila . . . Connie . . . Maggie. Front line, thank you very much, thank you, I'm sorry.

> (*Front line exits leaving the eight chosen:* CASSIE, VAL, DIANA, JUDY, MIKE, RICHIE, MARK *and* BOBBY. *After the eliminated have left the stage:*)

Rehearsals begin September 22nd. We'll rehearse for six weeks with a two-month out-of-town try-out. Our New York opening will be sometime mid-January. Be prepared to sign a Standard Minimum Contract with a six-month rider. You'll be contacted sometime next week as to where and when to sign your contract. And I'm very glad we're going to be working together.

(Piano fades as lights fade. Lights have dimmed to black by the end of the speech)

FINALE—BOWS

BOYS *(Plus offstage boys; sing)*:

ONE SINGULAR SENSATION
EV'RY LITTLE STEP HE TAKES.
ONE THRILLING COMBINATION
EV'RY MOVE THAT HE MAKES.
ONE SMILE AND SUDDENLY NOBODY ELSE WILL DO;
YOU KNOW YOU'LL NEVER BE LONELY WITH YOU KNOW WHO.

ONE MOMENT IN HIS PRESENCE
AND YOU CAN FORGET THE REST.
FOR THE GUY IS SECOND BEST
TO NONE,
SON.
OOOOH! SIGH! GIVE HIM YOUR ATTENTION.
DO . . . I . . . REALLY HAVE TO MENTION?
HE'S THE ONE?

SHE WALKS INTO A ROOM
AND YOU KNOW

GIRLS *(Plus offstage girls)*:

SHE'S UN-
COMMONLY RARE, VERY UNIQUE,
PERIPATETIC, POETIC AND CHIC.

ALL (*Including offstage*):
SHE WALKS INTO A ROOM
AND YOU KNOW FROM HER
MADDENING POISE, EFFORTLESS WHIRL,
SHE'S THE SPECIAL GIRL.

STROLL-
ING,
CAN'T HELP
ALL OF HER QUALITIES
EXTOL-
LING.
LOADED WITH CHARISMA IS MA
JAUNTILY SAUNTERING, AMBLING SHAMBLER.

SHE WALKS INTO A ROOM
AND YOU KNOW YOU MUST
SHUFFLE ALONG, JOIN THE PARADE.
SHE'S THE QUINTESSENCE OF MAKING THE GRADE.
THIS IS WHATCHA CALL
TRAV'LING.
OH, STRUT YOUR STUFF!
CAN'T GET ENOUGH

OF
HER.
LOVE
HER.
I'M A SON OF A GUN,
SHE IS ONE OF A
KIND . . .

(*Mirror panels in*)

nale

BOYS:

  ONE
  SINGULAR SENSATION
  EV'RY LITTLE STEP SHE
  TAKES.
  ONE
  THRILLING COMBINATION
  EV'RY MOVE THAT SHE

  MAKES.

  ONE SMILE AND
  SUDDENLY NOBODY
  ELSE WILL
  DO.
  YOU KNOW YOU'LL
  NEVER BE LONELY WITH
  YOU KNOW
  WHO.

  ONE
  MOMENT IN HER PRESENCE
  AND YOU CAN FORGET THE

  REST.

  FOR THE GIRL IS SECOND
  BEST TO
  NONE,
  SON.

  OOH! SIGH!

GIRLS:

  SHE WALKS INTO A ROOM
  AND YOU KNOW SHE'S UN-
  COMMONLY RARE, VERY UNIQUE,
  PERIPATETIC, POETIC, AND CHIC.
  SHE WALKS INTO A ROOM
  AND YOU KNOW FROM HER
  MADDENING POISE, EFFORTLESS
    WHIRL,
  SHE'S THE SPECIAL GIRL.

  STROLL-
  ING,
  CAN'T HELP
  ALL OF HER QUALITIES
  EXTOL-
  LING.
  LOADED WITH CHARISMA IS MA
  JAUNTILY SAUNTERING, AMBLING
    SHAMBLER.

  SHE WALKS INTO A ROOM
  AND YOU KNOW YOU MUST
  SHUFFLE ALONG, JOIN THE
    PARADE.
  SHE'S THE QUINTESSENCE OF
    MAKING THE GRADE.
  THIS IS WHATCHA CALL
  TRAV'LING.
  OH, STRUT YOUR STUFF!
  CAN'T GET ENOUGH.

  OF

GIVE HER YOUR ATTENTION.   HER.
DO I   LOVE.
REALLY HAVE TO MENTION   HER.
SHE'S   I'M A SON OF A GUN,
THE   SHE IS ONE OF A
ONE? . . .   KIND . . .

    (*Ribbon-Deco panels in*)

ALL:

ONE SINGULAR SENSATION
EV'RY LITTLE STEP SHE TAKES.
ONE THRILLING COMBINATION
EV'RY MOVE THAT SHE MAKES.
ONE SMILE AND SUDDENLY NOBODY ELSE WILL DO.
YOU KNOW YOU'LL NEVER BE LONELY WITH YOU KNOW WHO.

ONE MOMENT IN HER PRESENCE
AND YOU CAN FORGET THE REST.
FOR THE GIRL IS SECOND BEST
TO NONE, SON.

    (*Mirror panels in*)

OOOH! SIGH! GIVE HER YOUR ATTENTION.
DO I REALLY HAVE TO MENTION
SHE'S THE . . .
SHE'S THE . . .
SHE'S THE . . .
ONE!

Lights fade on "Rockette" kick line. After the company has exited—mirror panels to black—the house lights slowly come up. After singers cut off, orchestra continues vamp phrase, very loud, until cut off cue from stage manager. There are no additional "Bows" after this—leaving the audience with an image of a kick line that goes on forever.